D1376737

Learning from the Past

How Canadian Fiscal Policies of the
1990s Can Be Applied Today

Niels Veldhuis, Jason Clemens,
and Milagros Palacios

Fraser Institute
www.fraserinstitute.org
2012

Date of issue: January 2012
Printed and bound in Canada

Cover design and artwork
Bill C. Ray

Library and Archives Canada Cataloguing in Publication Data

Learning from the past: How Canadian fiscal policies of the 1990s can be applied today / by Niels Veldhuis, Jason Clemens, and Milagros Palacios

Includes bibliographical references.
ISBN 978-0-88975-254-2.

Contents

Introduction

Those who do not remember the past are condemned to repeat it.

George Santayana

Like most developed countries, Canada is gradually emerging from the financial crisis and ensuing global recession that began in 2007. Most countries, including Canada, are struggling to rein in sizeable deficits and avoid debt crises while not jeopardizing economic recovery. Canada's federal government and many of the provincial governments have laid out plans to eliminate their deficits over the coming years. Unfortunately, the federal and many provincial plans are based on suspect assumptions about the economy over the next number of years: strong revenue growth (based on a strong economic recovery), restrained spending growth, and limited increases in interest rates. Rather than relying on questionable assumptions about the future, the federal and various provincial governments should have looked at their own experiences in the mid-1990s when Canada led the world in solving its deficit and debt problems. The principal aim of this book is to educate readers about the state of the current problems at the federal level, its parallels with the failures of the 1980s and early 1990s, how governments solved these problems in the mid-1990s, and how we can solve today's fiscal problems using those lessons.

In many ways, this is a study of the virtuous cycle that occurs when governments act promptly and deliberately to eliminate deficits, leading to surpluses and debt reduction, which allows interest costs to decline, leading to yet more surpluses and debt reduction, and so on. It also outlines the vicious cycle that can emerge, and emerge quickly, when deficits are not dealt with:

namely deficits that lead to accumulating debt, which necessitates increased interest costs, which lead to yet larger deficits, and so on.

This book relies heavily on graphic illustrations rather than lengthy exposition and we have attempted to keep the discussion to only the most salient and germane points. The book is divided into two part parts. The first part of the book examines federal finances. Chapter 1 examines the status quo of the federal government's fiscal plans, its risks, the government's expectations for the future, and the current plan to eliminate the deficit. Chapter 2 explains how the current circumstances mirror those experienced in the 1980s and early 1990s. The parallels between these two periods are important since they help us to understand what works and what does not. Chapter 3 highlights the historical reforms enacted by the federal government in the mid-1990s. These reforms resulted in balanced budgets, reduced debt, declining interest costs, and a generally prosperous economy. The fourth chapter outlines a series of reforms based on the experience and success of the 1990s designed to return the country to fiscal balance and prosperity.

The second part of the book examines provincial government finances. Almost all of the provinces[1] face ongoing deficits, mounting debt, interest costs crowding out real spending on programs, and rising spending pressures. Unfortunately, most of the provinces, like the federal government, have forgotten the lessons of the 1990s and are making the same mistakes observed prior to the 1990s reforms. Chapter 5 examines the state of provincial finances today, with specific attention paid to deficits, debt levels, interest costs, and government spending. Chapter 6 highlights how the current provincial circumstances mirror those of the 1980s and early 1990s. Chapter 7 presents an overview of the reforms undertaken by the provinces in the 1990s and summarizes the key lessons learned during that period. Chapter 8 provides some general recommendations and conclusions based on the evidence gleamed from the experience of the 1990s. As they do today, the provinces in the 1980s and early 1990s struggled with deficits, growing debt, and interest costs. This chapter summarizes and analyzes the situation faced by the provinces during this period as well as their response in the 1990s.

---

1   The term "provinces" is used throughout to refer to provincial governments.

Learning from the Past

Federal finances—understanding the successes of the 1990s and applying them today

Part I is based on *Budget Blueprint: How Lessons from Canada's 1995 Budget Can Be Applied Today* (Veldhuis, Clemens, and Palacios, 2011). It has been revised and updated to reflect the 2011 Budget passed in June 2011.

Chapter 1

Federal finances today

Canada has not been spared the costs and pain of the financial crisis and global recession. Like every other industrialized country Canada has experienced slow or even negative economic growth, increasing unemployment, and deficits. This chapter summarizes the current financial state of the federal government and presents the expectations for the future based on recent government budgets.[1]

Perhaps the most striking measure of the change in Canada's finances is the marked move from consistent surplus to deficit. Deficits and surpluses refer to the financial performance of the government in any single period, normally a fiscal year. A deficit occurs when the resources collected by the government as taxes and fees are less than the amount spent on direct programs, transfers, and debt charges. Figure 1 depicts the surpluses and deficits of the federal government as a percentage of the economy (GDP) starting in 1997/98, the first year in which the federal government recorded a surplus after the mid-1990s reforms.[2] It also includes the latest expectations for the government over the next five years (2015/16). As shown in figure 1, the federal government had surpluses in every year between 1997/98 and 2007/08. Canada was a world-leader during this period for its ability to balance its financial affairs.

---

1   The principal sources of information for the federal government's expectations for the future are the *Update on Economic and Fiscal Projections, October 2010* (Canada, Dep't of Finance, 2010d) and the recently passed federal budget, *Next Phase of Canada's Economic Action Plan—A Low-Tax Plan for Jobs and Growth* (June 6) (Canada, Dep't of Finance, Canada, 2011).

2   The federal government has an operating year that begins on April 1 and ends on March 30. The fiscal years for the federal government are written in this style: "2011/12." The provinces also operate on a split calendar year.

Figure 1: Federal deficit or surplus as a percentage of GDP, 1997/98–2015/16

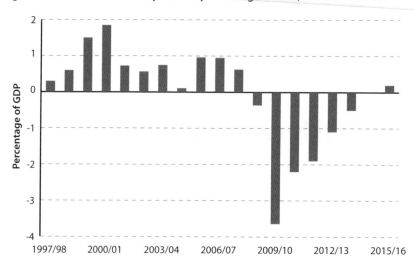

Note: Data for 2010/11 to 2015/16 are based on the federal government's most recent forecast and projections.
Sources: Canada, Department of Finance, 2010c, 2011.

Indeed no other OECD nation[3] managed to match or better Canada's performance over this period of time (*The Economist*, 2003, Sept. 25).

As the global recession took hold in 2008, Canada recorded a small deficit of $5.8 billion, representing 0.36% of GDP. This relatively small deficit in 2008/09 was largely due to revenues lower than expected: revenues were $5.5 billion lower in 2008/09 than originally budgeted the previous year (Canada, Dep't of Finance, 2009). The deficit for 2009/10 reached $55.6 billion or 3.6% of GDP. Almost one in four dollars spent by the federal government in 2009/10 on programs was borrowed. This historically high deficit in terms of dollar values was due, in part, to lower revenues: budget revenues for 2009/10 totaled $218.6 billion, lower than the originally expected $224.9 billion and much lower than the previous year's revenues of $233.1 billion.[4] The bulk of the deficit, however, is explained by the explosion in federal spending. Federal program spending increased to $244.8 billion in 2009/10 from $207.9 billion

---

3   The Organisation for Economic Co-operation and Development (OECD) is a group of 34 industrial countries. For more information, see <http://www.oecd.org>.
4   The references to original expectations in this section are based on the planned revenues and program spending included in the 2009 budget (Canada, Dep't of Finance, 2009) compared to actual results, as shown in the federal budget for 2011 (Canada, Dep't of Finance, 2011).

the previous year, an increase of 17.7% (see figure 5). It was also well above the level planned originally in the 2009 Budget, which indicated federal program spending of $224.9 billion.

As illustrated in figure 1, the federal government does not expect to return to a balanced budget or surplus position until 2015/16. The expected surplus in 2015/16 is $4.2 billion, 0.20% of GDP.[5] In other words, the government expects only a nominal surplus in 2015/16 and, in the meantime, expects to incur over $146.6 billion in debt between 2008/09, when it first began running a deficit, and 2015/16, when it expects to return to surplus.

Critically, the federal government has enacted a strategic and operating review of spending with a goal of saving $11 billion over four years beginning in 2012/13. Figure 2 illustrates the effect of the planned savings on total government spending (program and debt charges). Specifically, the federal government has targeted savings of $1 billion in 2012/13, $2 billion in 2013/14, and $4 billion in both 2014/15 and 2015/16 (figure 2). Put differently, the majority of the planned savings outlined by the government occurs in 2014/15 and 2015/16. The planned savings would enable the federal government to have a surplus one year earlier than currently planned, in 2014/15. However, savings from this process have not yet been identified and are not included in the government's forward plan for spending.[6]

Recall that a deficit refers to a period in which a government spends more than it collects in revenues. The result of deficits is debt, which is simply the accumulation of deficits over time.[7] Not surprising given the results presented in figure 1, Canada's national debt[8] is expected to increase.

---

5   A different way of thinking about the size of the expected surplus is as a share of expected revenues. The expected surplus of $4.2 billion in 2015/16 represents 1.4% of expected budget revenues.

6   For further information, see Canada, Dep't of Finance, 2011: table 5.2 (p. 185).

7   Debt can also be incurred outside deficits when long-term financing, such as bonds are issued to pay for long-term assets. For example, a government might determine that the building of a highway or bridge is in the long-term interest of its citizens. It issues long-term bonds to raise the resources needed to build the infrastructure and then subsequently pays back the bonds over time as the benefits from the infrastructure accrue. This is a situation in which government debt is accumulated outside the annual deficits or surpluses recorded by the government.

8   There are a variety of measures of debt available. For a number of reasons, including consistency, we have chosen to use a series referred to as "accumulated deficits," a series that measures gross or total debt minus financial and non-financial assets.

Figure 2: The effect of planned savings on overall federal government spending (nominal $ billions), 2010/11–2015/16

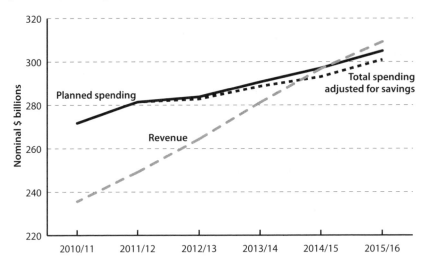

Note: Spending includes both program spending and debt charges.
Sources: Canada, Department of Finance, 2011.

Figure 3 illustrates the nominal value of Canada's federal debt from 2000/01 to the expectation for 2015/16. The marked increase in Canada's federal debt beginning in 2008/09 when deficits reappeared is unmistakable. Canada's debt has increased from a low of $457.6 billion in 2007/08 to $553.1 billion last year (2010/11). It is expected to reach a high of $614.5 billion by 2014/15 before starting to decline as the country enters budget surpluses. It is not an exaggeration to say that Canada's national debt has exploded over the last two years and will continue to balloon until leveling off in 2013/14.[9]

Fortunately, the increase in the country's federal debt has been less dramatic when compared to the size of the economy. Debt as a share of GDP is an important measure since recent research has demonstrated the serious costs imposed on economies in the form of slower economic growth and the risks of financial crises when government debt reaches certain thresholds.[10] Federal

---

9 Relatively small increases in the nominal value of the national debt are recorded in 2013/14 and 2014/15.

10 Reinhart and Rogoff, 2009. Reinhart and Rogoff have published numerous studies and papers examining the economics of debt and financial crises. This publication succinctly summarizes much of that research. See also Kumar and Woo, 2010.

Figure 3: Federal debt (nominal $ billions), 2000/01–2015/16

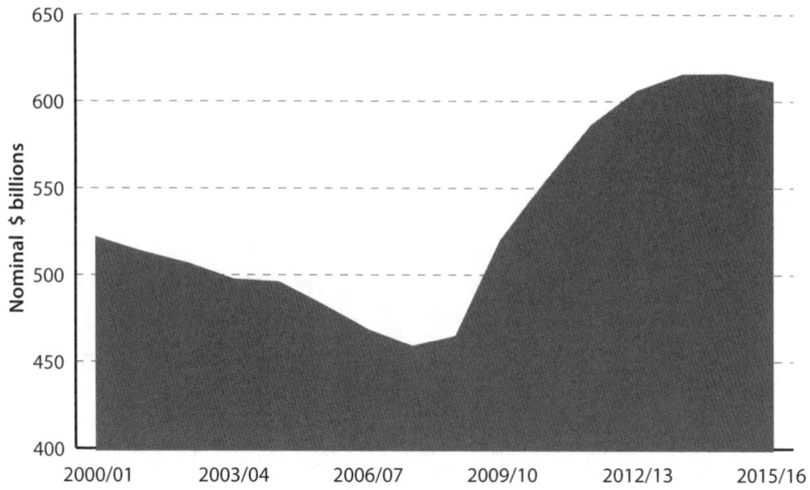

Notes: Data for 2010/11 to 2015/16 are based on the federal government's most recent forecast and projections. There are several series available for measuring federal debt. The series chosen for this study is accumulated deficits, which measures gross or total debt minus financial and non-financial assets.
Sources: Canada, Department of Finance, 2010c: tables 1, 2; 2011.

debt as a share of the economy (GDP) reached a low of 29.0% in 2008/09. It is expected to increase to a high of 34.3% in 2011/12 before starting to decline based on renewed economic growth (Canada, Dep't of Finance, 2010c: tables 1, 2; 2011). Recall that the value of the nominal federal debt will continue to increase until 2015/16.

One of the costs of deficits and the related increase in debt is higher interest costs. Interest charges are simply the interest payments made on the stock of existing debt. They do not include payments that reduce the amount of outstanding debt. Interest charges on the country's federal debt are expected to increase over the next five years. Federal interest charges hit a low of $29.4 billion in 2009/10. They have since increased and are expected to reach $39.4 billion in 2014/15, an increase of 34.0%. Indeed, the latest federal government projections indicate that interest costs will continue to increase over the entirety of the government's budgeting period (figure 4).

It is important to understand what is referred to as the "wedge effect" of interest costs. Interest charges create a wedge between what a government collects in resources (that is, taxes and fees) and what the government actually spends on programs and services. The best measure available to gauge

Figure 4: Federal interest charges (nominal $ billions), 2000/01–2015/16

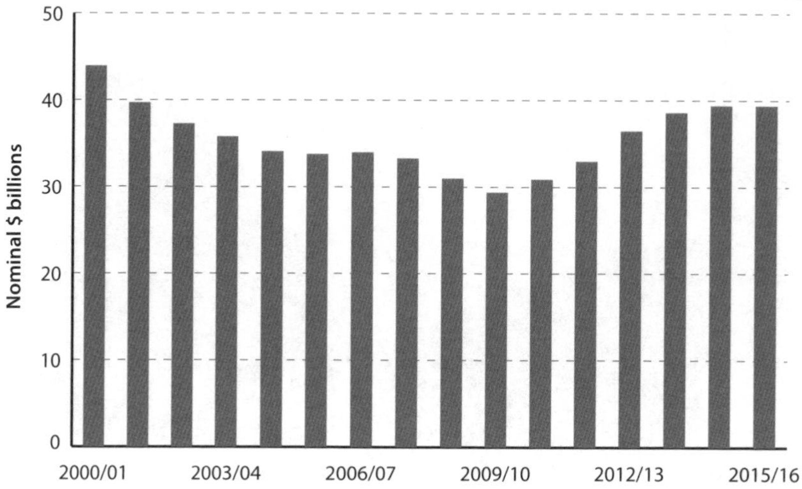

Note: Data for 2010/11 to 2015/16 are based on the federal government's most recent forecast and projections.
Sources: Canada, Department of Finance, 2010c, 2010d, 2011; Canada, Receiver General for Canada, 2010.

this wedge between revenues and actual spending on programs is to examine interest charges as a share of budget revenues.

The share of budget revenues dedicated to interest costs steadily declined beginning in the late 1990s until 2009/10 when they started to increase (figure 23b). More specifically, interest charges as a percentage of revenues reached a low of 13.3% in 2008/09 before starting to increase, albeit slightly. They are expected to peak in 2012/13 at 13.8% of revenues. This upward trend is expected to continue until 2013/14 based on the federal government's current GDP and interest rate assumptions. Specifically, nominal interest costs are expected to rise throughout this period (figure 4) but the current budget assumes revenues will grow faster than interest costs, thus reducing the effect of higher interest costs. However, if the current assumptions about interest rates and GDP growth prove overly optimistic, the wedge between the resources collected and what is available for spending could easily increase.

Thus far we have outlined the state of the current deficit, the federal expectation of returning to surplus in 2015/16, and the implications of deficits on debt and interest costs. To understand the nature of the government's plan to return to surplus, we now examine government spending and revenue expectations for the next five years. Figure 5 illustrates federal spending, both program and total spending, beginning in 2000/01.[11]

There are two important facts here. One, both program and total spending have been increasing almost without pause since 2000/01. Indeed, even before the recession hit in 2008/09, program spending had increased from $130.6 billion in 2000/01 to $207.9 billion in 2008/09, an increase of almost 60% in less than a decade. The government expects program spending to reach $265.6 billion in 2015/16, which is more than double the amount spent in 2000/01.The second important fact is the presence of the "fiscal stimulus" in 2009/10.[12] Program spending increased by $36.9 billion (17.7%) in that year alone. The intent of the federal government was to combat the recession through traditional Keynesian methods, that is, through a combination of increased government spending (purchases) and tax relief designed to stimulate consumer spending.[13]

An overlooked aspect of figure 5—and one we shall return to later—is the absence of any meaningful or sustained decline in spending.[14] If you examine either program or total spending after 2009/10, you may notice a decline in the growth of spending but not an actual reduction in spending except for the small reduction in 2010/11, which is offset by the increase in 2011/12.[15] Stimulus spending, which, by design, is meant to be temporary would require a return to normal spending after the money allocated for stimulus is exhausted. However, the spending profile shown in figure 5 indicates that the stimulus spending looks like simply more permanent spending over time rather than a one-time or temporary increase in spending.

---

11 It is important to recognize that program spending is at the discretion of the government while total spending is partially driven by factors out of its control. Specifically, total spending includes interest charges, whose nominal value is determined by market forces.

12 For information about the federal stimulus plan, see Canada, Dep't of Finance, 2010b; and TD Economics, 2009.

13 For a discussion of the effectiveness of the federal government's stimulus spending, see Karabegović, Lammam, and Veldhuis, 2010.

14 This analysis excludes the proposed savings—$11 billion in total—from the strategic and operating review of spending initiated by the federal government. It expects to save $11 billion beginning in 2012/13, which will result in a balanced budget in 2014/15, one year earlier than currently planned.

15 Program spending is scheduled to decline by $7.6 billion (3.2%) and total spending is forecast to decline by $9.7 billion (3.6%) in 2011/12 (Canada, Dep't of Finance, 2011).

Figure 5: Federal total and program spending (nominal $ billions), 2000/01–2015/16

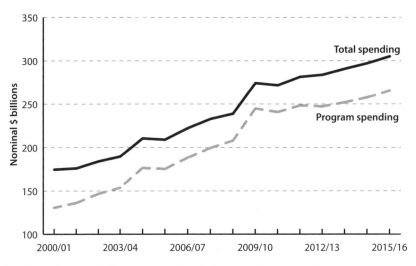

Note: Data for 2010/11 to 2015/16 are based on the federal government's most recent forecast and projections.
Sources: Canada, Department of Finance, 2010c, 2010d, 2011; Canada, Receiver General for Canada, 2010.

Figure 6 places federal spending in the context of the economy: it presents federal program and total spending as a percentage of GDP. The effect of the 2009/10 stimulus plan is even more evident here. Program spending increases from 13.0% of GDP in 2008/09 to 16.0% of GDP in 2009/10.

The government expects both total and program spending to decline as a share of the economy over the next five years. However, neither total nor program spending will return to its pre-stimulus share of the economy (14.9% and 13.0%) until 2015/16. Critically, and not readily clear in figure 6, is that this achievement is not due to spending reductions. Recall from figure 5 that spending, both total and program, does not decline over the next five years. Instead, its rate of growth is slowed. The reduction in spending as a share of the economy is entirely a function of reducing the growth in spending coupled with stronger GDP growth rather than actually reducing nominal spending.

As will be discussed later, this reliance on stronger GDP growth and related growth in budget revenues rather than direct action by the government to reduce spending is the Achilles' heel of the federal government's current plan. Figure 7 compares the annual growth in program spending to the change in population and inflation in the same year, illustrating the

Figure 6: Federal total and program spending (percentage of GDP), 2000/01–2015/16

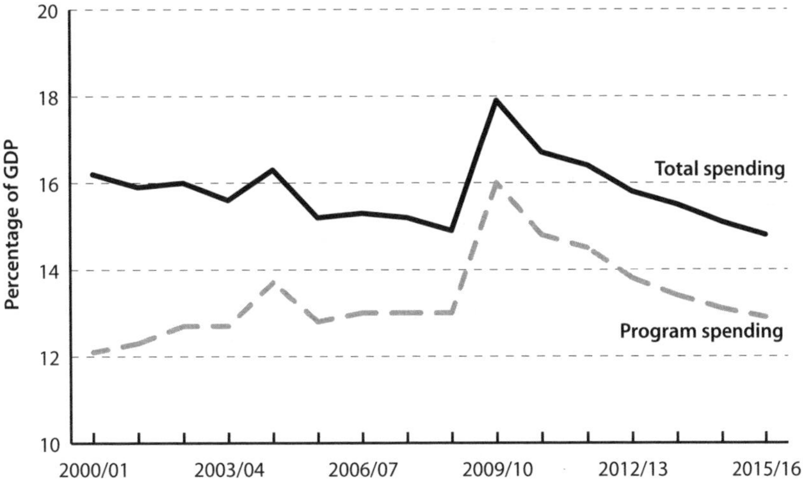

Note: Data for 2010/11 to 2015/16 are based on the federal government's most recent forecast and projections.
Sources: Canada, Department of Finance, 2010c, 2010d, 2011; Canada, Receiver General for Canada, 2010.

difference between how much program spending actually increased and what was required to accommodate for increases in prices and population.

It is important to understand figure 7 by breaking the period into two sections, pre-stimulus (2009/10) and post-stimulus. Before the federal government enacted the stimulus package of 2009/10, government program spending had increased faster than population growth and increases in prices in every year except 2005/06. In other words, in seven of the eight years between 2001/02 and the stimulus of 2009/10, government program spending increased faster than population and inflation.[16] Fiscal year 2009/10 is obviously unique because of the marked increase in spending based on the stimulus program. The government's plan for the future is for program spending to increase at a rate less than population growth and inflation in four of the six years.[17] Specifically, program spending grows less than population

---

16 For a discussion of the relationship between government spending and economic performance, see Alesina, Ardagna, Perotti, and Schiantarelli, 2002; Alesina, Perotti, Giavazzi, and Kollintzas, 1995.
17 To some extent, however, the federal government has already signaled a willingness to review existing spending in order to restrain the nominal growth in spending and achieve improved results (see Canada, Dep't of Finance, 2009).

Figure 7: Growth in federal spending compared to growth in population plus change in the Consumer Price Index (CPI), 2001/02–2015/16

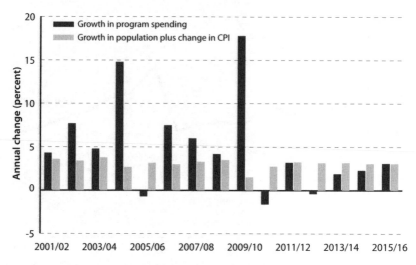

Notes: Population growth was forecast at 10-year average of 1.06% growth rate. Data for 2010/11 to 2015/16 are based on the federal government's most recent forecast and projections.

Sources: Canada, Department of Finance, 2010c, 2010d, 2011; Canada, Receiver General for Canada, 2010; Statistics Canada 2010c; calculations by the authors.

and inflation in 2010/11 (last year), and from 2012/13 to 2014/15. Program spending is planned to exceed the rate of population growth and inflation in 2015/16 and is basically at the same level in 2011/12.

The key to the federal government's plan is slowing the growth in spending over the next five years. This can be seen in the latter half of figure 7, where spending growth is constrained. One major risk to this plan is obvious: if spending growth is not sufficiently constrained, the government will fail to reach its fiscal objectives. One can envision numerous scenarios where it would be prohibitively difficult for the government to constrain spending growth, such as an election call.

The key objective the federal government has set out is returning to a balanced budget or surplus by 2015/16. Figure 8 illustrates the achievement of that objective by comparing budget revenues and total spending, both actual to date and those planned for the future. The achievement of a balanced budget in 2015/16 is the result of two principal factors. The first, a slowdown in the growth of spending by the federal government, has already been discussed. This can be seen in the flattening of the spending line in figure 8 after 2009/10.

Figure 8: Federal revenues and spending (nominal $ billions), 2000/01–2015/16

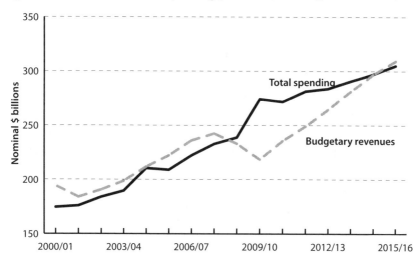

Note: Data for 2010/11 to 2015/16 are based on the federal government's most recent forecast and projections.
Sources: Canada, Department of Finance, 2010c, 2010d, 2011; Canada, Receiver General for Canada, 2010.

The second contributing factor is the rebound of budget revenues beginning in 2010/11. The steep recovery in budget revenues based on strong economic growth allows the federal government to achieve a balanced budget in five years while still increasing spending over that time period. Clearly, there is a second major risk to the federal government's plan: it relies on a strong rebound in the growth of GDP and budget revenues that may not materialize.[18]

Conclusion

The federal government is experiencing sizeable budget deficits, which are leading to the accumulation of debt and increasing interest costs. The current deficit is a function of reduced revenues and, to a much greater extent, higher spending. Indeed, spending increases by the federal government had been sizeable for many years even before the crisis of 2008. More importantly, the

18 Interestingly, table 2.1 in the *Update of Economic and Financial Projections, October 2010* (Canada, Dep't of Finance, 2010d) shows downward revisions for both nominal and real GDP in 2011, 2012, and 2013. The estimates for 2013 and 2014 showed a mix of stable and moderately increasing expectations.

one-time, temporary stimulus spending seems to have been simply folded into permanent spending in the future. In other words, the government's spending plans do not show spending returning to its pre-stimulus levels, even after adjusting for growth in the population and increases in prices.

The government's plan to return to balance is to slow the growth of federal spending over the next five years and allow revenues to catch up as the economy recovers. That is, the government assumes it can restrain spending growth for the next five years while the economy experiences strong GDP growth that will result in higher revenues. The risks of such an approach are clear: some combination of failure to slow increases in spending, lower-than-expected GDP growth and revenues, and higher-than-expected interest costs could all derail the government's plan and leave the federal government in an on-going deficit position.

Chapter 2

Déjà vu—Canada has been here before

Part of the disappointment with the federal government's current plan to solve the deficit is that it appears to ignore its own recent history. Canada faced a more serious fiscal situation for the better part of a decade and a half before real reforms were enacted in 1995. Those reforms, however, were materially different from the plan laid out by the current federal government. Indeed, part of the inability of the federal government to solve the problem in the 1980s and early 1990s was that it relied on a similar plan to the one being used now. This chapter details the problems faced by the federal government throughout the 1980s and early 1990s and how successive governments failed to solve these problems.

Figure 9 presents the deficit position of the federal government as a share of the economy (GDP) from 1980/81 to 1995/96 (year of reform). There was no year in this period in which the federal government recorded a surplus. In dollar terms, the deficit ranged from a low of $14.6 billion in 1980/81 to a high of $39.0 billion in 1992/93 (Canada, Dep't of Finance, 2010c). In comparison, the nominal deficit in 2009/10 was $55.6 billion (Canada, Dep't of Finance, 2010d). As a share of the economy, the federal deficit ranged from a low of 4.4% of GDP in 1981/82 to a high of 8.3% of GDP in 1984/85. The deficit in 2009/10 was 3.6% of GDP. So, although the dollar value of the deficit in 2009/10 was substantially above the highest level incurred during the 1980s and early 1990s, as a share of the economy it was actually much smaller, which should allow the government to eliminate the deficit more easily than was the case in the mid-1990s.

Figure 9: Federal deficit (percentage of GDP), 1980/81–1995/96

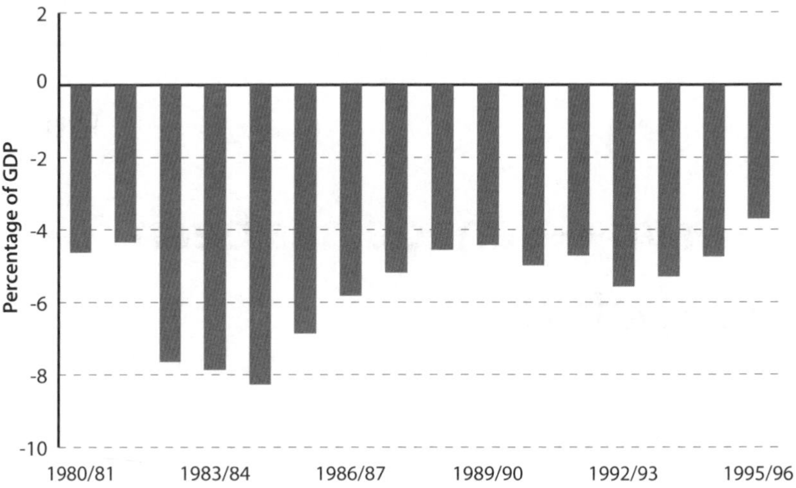

Source: Canada, Department of Finance, 2010c.

Given the enormous deficits recorded by the federal government during the 1980s and early 1990s, it should come as no surprise that there was a marked increase in the federal debt. In dollar terms, the federal debt increased from $227.8 billion in 1985/86 to $554.2 billion in 1995/96 (Canada, Dep't of Finance, 2010c). Figure 10 presents the value of the federal debt as a share of GDP beginning in 1985/86.[1] Federal debt as a share of the economy increased from 46.9% in 1985/86, which was bad enough, to 68.4% in 1995/96. Indeed, the run-up in the federal debt over this time period is almost a straight line without any interruption. This increase in the federal debt is important to understand in the light of emerging research concerning the economic effects of government debt.[2] Recent research by Carmen M. Reinhart (University of Maryland) and Kenneth S. Rogoff (Harvard University) on the economics of debt accumulation by government indicates a threshold of debt accumulation of 90% of GDP, after which economies tend to experience slower economic growth and related costs. This threshold is important because in 1995/96 the

---

1   The series used for debt is not available on a consistent basis before 1983/84 due to a change in accounting.

2   See chap. 1, footnote 10 for references to recent research on the economics of debt accumulation by government.

Figure 10: Federal debt (percentage of GDP), 1985/86–1995/96

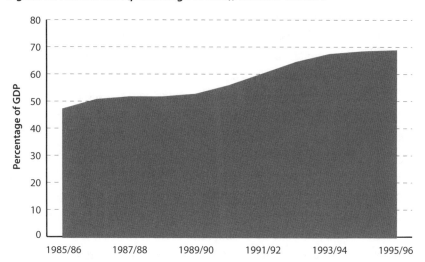

Notes: Data for 2010/11 to 2015/16 are based on the federal government's most recent forecast and projections for the future. There are several series available for measuring federal debt. The series chosen for this study is accumulated deficits, which measures gross or total debt minus financial and non-financial assets.
Source: Canada, Department of Finance, 2010c: tables 1 and 2.

federal government's debt-to-GDP ratio of 68.4% combined with the consolidated provincial debt-to-GDP ratio of 27.6% (Canada, Dep't of Finance, 2010c) meant that, even before municipal and other government debt was included, the country's debt had exceeded the threshold identified by Reinhart and Rogoff as likely to impair economic growth.[3]

As the national debt expanded so too did the costs of maintaining the debt: interest costs. In fact, the situation was made worse since interest rates themselves were generally increasing for much of the decade. Figure 11a shows the nominal value of the federal government's interest costs between 1980/81 and 1995/96. The nominal interest costs faced by the federal government increased from $10.7 billion in 1980/81 to $45.0 billion in 1990/91

---

3   On a national accounts basis, the total liabilities of the federal, provincial, and local governments as of 2009 totaled $1,643 billion; this included $775.1 billion in federal liabilities and $864.9 billion in provincial and local liabilities (Canada, Dep't of Finance, 2010c: tables 48, 49, 51). In addition, see *Canadian Government Debt 2008: A Guide to the Indebtedness of Canada and the Provinces* (Palacios, Veldhuis, and Harischandra, 2008), the Fraser Institute's cataloging study of government liabilities and its discussion of government enterprise (GBE) debt and other indirect types of liabilities such as debt guarantees.

before starting to decrease slightly as interest rates declined. Interest costs started to increase again, however, in 1994/95 as international capital markets began to re-assess the riskiness of Canadian government debt. For comparative purposes, nominal interest costs in 2009/10 were $29.4 billion and rising (Canada, Dep't of Finance, 2010c).

Recall that interest costs create a wedge between the resources collected by government as taxes and fees and the amount of those resources the government is able to spend on programs and services. As illustrated in figure 11b, the share of revenues spent on interest costs increased from an already worrying 20.0% in 1980/81 to 37.6% in 1990/91. Even after the slight declines observed in the early 1990s, interest costs still generally consumed more than one third of revenues up to 1995/96. The enormity of the problems associated with having one third of the resources collected allocated to interest costs cannot be overemphasized. Indeed, this is one of the key factors of the historic reforms enacted in 1995.

One of the benefits of the reforms in the 1990s has been that, even as the federal government entered deficits again in recent years, interest costs as a share of revenues have remained well below the levels observed in the 1990s. In 2009/10, for instance, interest costs only consumed 13.5% of budget revenues (figure 4). This affords the federal government more latitude than was the case in the 1980s and 1990s. However, that flexibility should be used to solve the problem more quickly rather than taking the slower approach the federal government has chosen.

Figure 12 illustrates federal total and program spending over the same time period, 1980/81 to 1995/96. What is abundantly clear is that even though the federal government was facing constant deficits, accumulating debt, and alarming interest costs, both program and total spending continued to increase throughout this period(Canada, Dep't of Finance, 2010c).

Figure 13 compares the annual growth rates in both total and program spending by the federal government to the increase in population and changes in prices. There are two periods in figure 13. The first runs from 1980/81 to 1984/85 (or so) and was characterized by fairly high rates of inflation. In only one year during this period did the growth in program spending not exceed the rate of population growth and inflation. Indeed, in many years the gap between the increases in spending and the rate of population

Figure 11a: Federal interest charges (nominal $ billions), 1980/81–1995/96

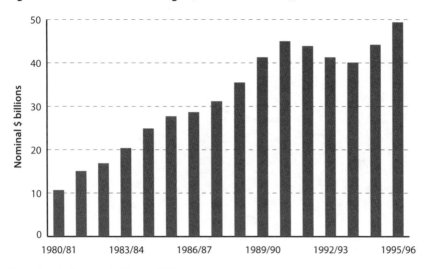

Source: Canada, Department of Finance, 2010c.

Figure 11b: Federal interest charges (percentage of budget revenues), 1980/81–1995/96

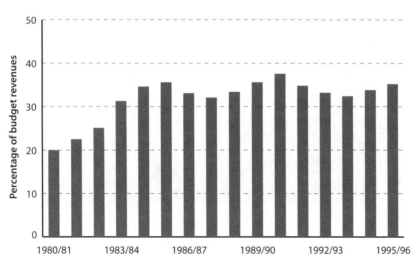

Source: Canada, Department of Finance, 2010c; calculations by authors.

Figure 12: Federal total and program spending (nominal $ billions), 1980/81–1995/96

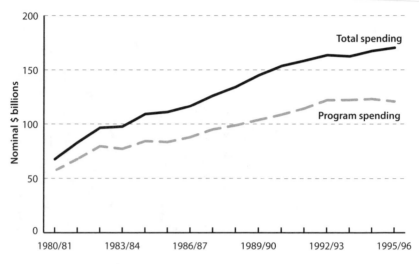

Source: Canada, Department of Finance, 2010c.

Figure 13: Growth in federal spending compared to growth in population plus change in the Consumer Price Index (CPI), 1980/81–1995/96

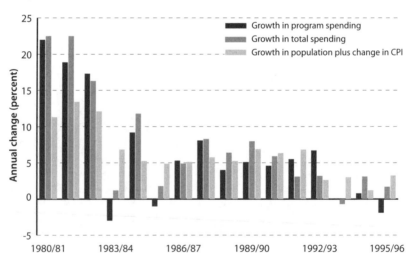

Sources: Canada, Department of Finance, 2010c; Statistics Canada, 2010a, 2010c; calculations by authors.

Figure 14: Federal revenues and spending (nominal $ billions), 1980/81–1995/96

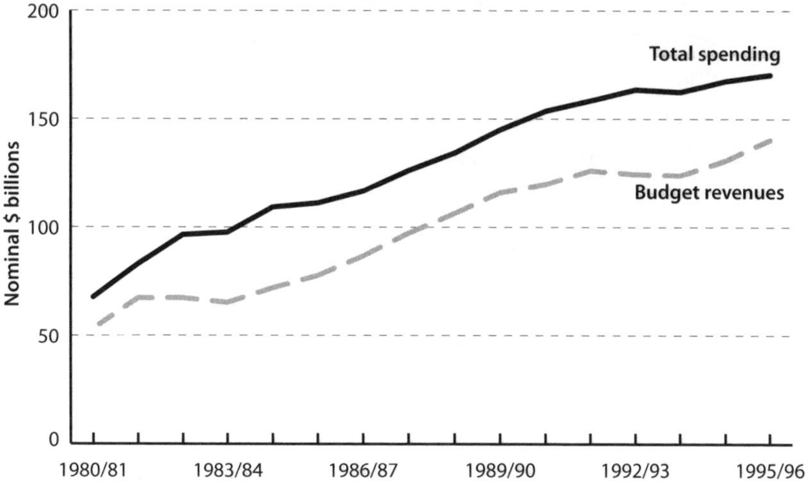

Source: Canada, Department of Finance, 2010c.

growth and inflation were substantial. For example, the growth in both total and program spending in 1980/81 was almost double the rate of population growth and inflation.

The second period begins in 1985/86 and was characterized by lower rates of inflation. The growth in both total and program spending during this period was much closer to the rates of population growth and inflation. There were also many years in which spending growth was constrained during this period. However, the restraint was not consistent.

This period was characterized by sizeable deficits. Figure 14 shows that throughout this period budget revenues grew but that their growth was insufficient to catch up with the annual growth in spending. Indeed, the gap or the size of the deficit actually increased over this time period.

So the question remains, then, why the federal government could not make greater progress in closing the deficit gap over this time period. The question is made even more perplexing given that the government of the day (the Progressive Conservative Party) was at least notionally predisposed to lower levels of government spending and balanced budgets. Part of the answer to this question is the increasing interest rates and consequent increasing interest costs that have already been addressed in this chapter. However, this overlooks a critically important reason for the government's failure to deal effectively with the deficit. Put simply, the plan used by the government to address the deficit was flawed. Rather than actually reducing spending in any meaningful way, the government chose to try to slow the growth in spending while hoping for strong revenue growth. This is exactly the same approach upon which the current federal government is relying.

Figure 15 shows the budget revenue expectations of the federal government in each of the budgets between 1984 and 1987. In four budget periods, there were two fairly marked reductions in the expectations of revenues. In other words, the federal government had to lower its expectations twice in terms of what it expected to collect in budget revenues over this four-year budget period. For example, between the 1984 and 1985 budgets, the federal government reduced its four-year revenue forecast by $11.5 billion. Put differently, over a four-year period from 1983/84 to 1986/87, the federal government expected to collect $11.5 billion less in its 1985 budget than it did in the previous 1984 budget. A similar, though smaller, reduction of revenue expectations occurred between the 1986 and 1987 budgets.

Interestingly, even as revenues did rebound and revenue expectations increased, the federal government was still unable to move closer to a balanced budget. The main reason for this failure is captured in figure 16, which presents the revised government estimates for total spending based on successive budgets from 1983 through to 1989. There is an undeniable trend: in each successive budget, the expectation for total spending in each fiscal year is always either stable or increased. The federal government experienced tremendous difficulty in constraining spending growth effectively and, even as revenues grew, they were not able to catch up with their higher spending level. The result was on-going deficits.

Conclusion

The parallels between the situations faced today and in the 1980s and 1990s are striking. In both periods, the federal government faced deficits and increasing debt coupled with increasing interest costs and the pressures those increases impose on government. Indeed, the pressures faced by the federal government in the 1980s and early 1990s were greater than is currently the case. Perhaps

Figure 15: Revised estimates for federal budget revenues (nominal $ billions), 1984–1987 Budgets

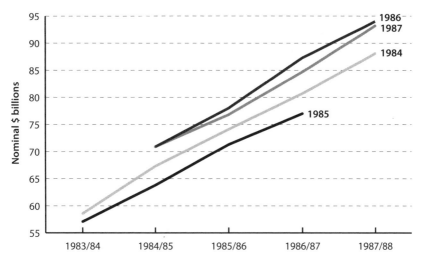

Sources: Canada, Department of Finance, 1984, 1985, 1986, 1987.

Figure 16: Revised estimates for federal total spending (nominal $ billions), 1983/84–1989/90 Budgets

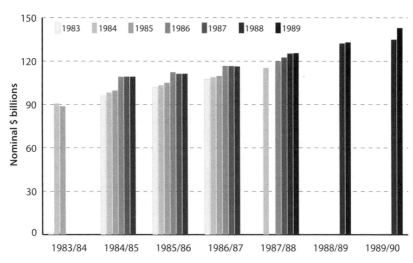

Sources: Canada, Department of Finance, 1984, 1985, 1986, 1987.

most importantly, both governments have implemented plans to solve the deficits based on constraining the growth in spending over time coupled with assumptions of stronger revenue growth rather than actually reducing spending. The failure of the government's plan in the 1980s and 1990s came from an inability to constrain spending growth coupled with lower than expected revenues. The failure of the government's approach to solving its fiscal problems meant on-going deficits, mounting debt, and increasing interest costs.

Chapter 3

Understanding federal successes of the 1990s

Jean Chretien's Liberal Party was swept into office in 1993.[1] Their first budget (1994) is generally considered a budget that held the status quo and one that did not undertake the difficult steps needed to rein in the deficit (Richards, 2000).[2] The financial situation the government faced in fiscal 1994/95 was daunting. The deficit had reached $36.6 billion, representing 4.75% of GDP and the debt had reached $524.2 billion or 68.0% of GDP. Interest costs paid by the government on the national debt reached $44.2 billion, consuming 33.8% of budget revenues. The deteriorating finances of the government coupled with a number of other factors motivated (some argue, forced) the government into action. It is worth describing those other factors to understand the circumstances within which historic reform occurred.

Politically, a unified, ideologically coherent, opposition in the form of Preston Manning's Reform Party was instrumental in establishing a parliamentary environment receptive to and supportive of many of the fiscal reforms proposed and enacted by the governing Liberals. In addition, a broad array of think tanks, advocacy groups, and business organizations had been educating the public on the risks and costs of the deficit and debt, such that the general public increasingly supported change. Reforms implemented in

---

1   For elections results, see <http://www.parl.gc.ca/Parlinfo/Files/Parliament.aspx?Item=421af128-812f-4cfb-a018-6ff7 6ce7a98e&Language=E&Section=PartyStandingsHOC>.

2   While the 1994 Budget did not include measures to tackle the deficit, it did establish a broad review process that would turn out to be critical in the subsequent 1995 Budget, since it included a commitment to "review" every government agency and program over the course of 1994 with an eye towards ensuring appropriate "size, scope, composition and cost. (Martin, 1994: 13).

Saskatchewan by Roy Romanow's NDP government and in Alberta by Ralph Klein's Conservatives created some political consensus regarding the need and efficacy of change.[3]

Externally, the collapse of the Mexican Peso in 1994 provided real-world evidence of the costs of ignoring deficits and debt. An editorial in the *Wall Street Journal* that commented on Canada's debt problem and suggested the country was nearing bankruptcy caused a sharp decline in the value of the Canadian dollar (1995, Jan. 12).[4] Interest rates were rising throughout the year and there was increasing concern about Canada's fiscal situation. International organizations such the International Monetary Fund and the Organisation for Economic Co-operation and Development (OECD) were calling for faster reductions in the country's deficit (Beauchesne, 1994, Dec. 6). These and other factors culminated in the delivery of the Liberal Party's 1995 budget, which is one of the most important budgets in modern Canadian history.

1995 budget—announcing and implementing historic reforms

The 1995 budget set in motion fundamental fiscal reforms and ultimately became a defining moment in Canada's fiscal history. In his budget speech, Finance Minister Paul Martin boldly articulated a new direction for the government: "We are acting on a new vision of the role of government ... smaller government ... smarter government" (Martin, 1995: 2). Importantly, the Finance Minister put the issue of the deficit in non-partisan terms by stating that "[t]he debt and deficit are not inventions of ideology. They are facts of arithmetic. The quicksand of compound interest is real" (Martin, 1995: 2)·

Table 1 summarizes the fiscal plan proposed in the 1995 budget. Unlike previous attempts to tackle the deficit—and unlike the approach of the current government—the governing Liberal Party planned to reduce nominal spending. The plan called for a reduction of program spending from $118.3 billion in 1994/95 to $107.9 billion in 1996/97. The government proposed

---

3   For a more thorough discussion of the reforms implemented in Saskatchewan and Alberta as well as in Ontario, see chapter 4, Fiscal Reform: Unsung Provincial Heroes, in Crowley, Clemens, and Veldhuis, 2010.

4   Then associate deputy minister of finance and later Governor of the Bank of Canada, David Dodge, called the *Wall Street Journal*'s editorial a "seminal event" (cited in Savoie, 1999: 178).

Table 1: Fiscal Outlook presented in the 1995 federal budget

	1994/95	1995/96	1996/97
$ billions			
Revenue	125.0	133.2	137.4
Program spending	118.3	114.0	107.9
Debt charges	42.0	49.5	50.7
Total spending	160.3	163.5	158.6
Deficit	37.9	32.7	24.3
Percent of GDP			
Revenue	16.7	16.9	16.7
Program spending	16.2	14.5	13.1
Deficit	5.1	4.2	3.0

Notes: Numbers may not add due to rounding or the exclusion of other relatively minor line items. Data for 1994/95 are preliminary estimates. 1995/96 and 1996/97 are forecasts.
Source: Canada, Department of Finance, 1995b.

cutting program spending by $10.4 billion, a decline of 8.8% over a two-year period. The budget also reduced public sector employment by 45,000 or 14%.

As illustrated in figure 17,[5] the government not only achieved its plan but exceeded it. Over two years (1995/96 and 1996/97), the federal government reduced program spending by $11.9 billion, a cut in spending of 9.7%. Again, this was not a slowing of growth in spending over time but rather a reduction in the amount of spending.

Importantly, the government also constrained the growth in spending after 1997/98 for three additional years. Figure 18 compares the growth in total and program spending with the rate of growth in population and inflation. What is evident is that the federal government not only cut spending in 1995/96 and 1996/97 but continued to constrain the growth of spending compared to population growth and inflation through to 1999/2000. Beginning in 2000/01 through to the remainder of the years covered in figure 18, the federal government allowed spending, particularly program spending, to grow at rates well in excess of the growth of the population and inflation.

---

5   Note that the figures included in table 1 reflect budgeted or planned spending rather than the actual spending numbers used in figure 17.

Figure 17: Federal total and program spending (nominal $ billions), 1994/95–2003/04

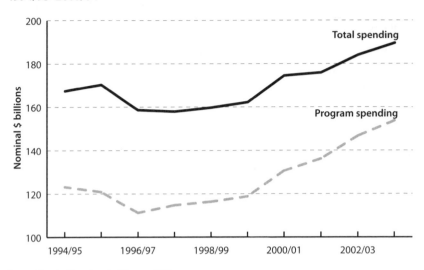

Source: Canada, Department of Finance, 2010c.

Figure 18: Growth in federal spending compared to growth in population plus change in the Consumer Price Index (CPI), 1995/96–2003/04

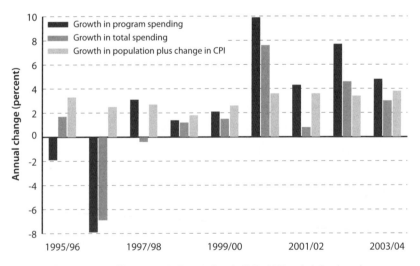

Sources: Canada, Department of Finance, 2010c; Statistics Canada, 2010a, 2010c; calculations by authors.

However, the critical point from the perspective of this study is what the Liberal government achieved from 1995/96 to 1999/2000.

A critical aspect of the reductions in spending was the concurrent reduction in the size of government compared to the economy.[6] Figure 19 illustrates the decline in federal total and program spending as a share of GDP the economy over this period. Specifically, federal program spending decreased from 16.0% of GDP in 1994/95 to a low of 12.1% of GDP by 2000/01. It then increased slightly to 13.7% in 2004/05. Total spending decreased from 21.7% of GDP in 1994/95 to 15.3% of GDP in 2005/06.

Getting government right—program review

Unlike other governments that have tackled deficits by cutting spending across the board, the federal government relied on a methodical approach aimed at prioritizing spending so that important areas were spared deep cuts while areas of less importance carried a greater burden for the reduction in spending. The theme of the approach echoed the words of the Finance Minister's speech in which he called for smaller, smarter government (Martin, 1995).

The prioritization process used by the federal government was referred to as the "Program Review." It was a comprehensive examination of federal departmental spending included in the 1994 budget. The review required ministers in each department to evaluate their programs using six tests:

1. serving the public interest
2. necessity of government involvement
3. appropriate federal role
4. scope for public-sector–private-sector partnerships
5. scope for increased efficiency, and
6. affordability.

The Program Review led to a significant structural change in the federal government's involvement in the Canadian economy, including:

---

6   For a recent summary of the research on the economics of the size of government, see Clemens, Veldhuis, and Kaszton, 2010.

Figure 19: Federal total and program spending (percentage of GDP), 1994/95–2005/06

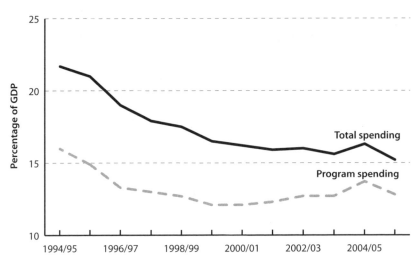

Source: Canada, Department of Finance, 2010c.

- changes to the federal government's involvement in large aspects of Canada's transportation system;[7]
- a complete change to the federal government's approach to agriculture, including a move away from income support to income stabilization;[8]
- a reduction in the federal government's involvement in the business sector, including a proposed 60% cut in business subsidies;[9]
- an increased focus on efficiency in government departments and the manner in which they delivered services to Canadians.

---

7 There was a marked shift in the role and responsibilities of Transport Canada. Instead of owning, operating, and subsidizing the transportation system, Transport Canada move to a role of developing policies, regulating transportation, and enforcing safety standards. Some of the reforms included transferring airport management and, indeed, ownership to local authorities, privatizing the Air Navigation System (NavCan), and eliminating subsidies for farmers and transportation companies.

8 The 1995 Budget included measures to reduce federal support of agricultural safety nets by 30% over three years, cuts to subsidies to milk producers of 30% over two years, reductions in federal spending on inspection and regulation, the closing of seven research facilities, and ending the Feed Freight Assistance transportation subsidy.

9 Resources remaining for supporting business would largely be in the form of loans and repayable contributions rather than subsidies.

Table 2 summarizes the reductions proposed for various departments through the Program Review process. The results clearly show a prioritization of then-existing spending. Some departments were required to implement large reductions in spending, including Transport (51%), Natural Resources (49%), Agriculture (40%), and Industry (43%). Other departments were asked to implement fairly small reductions, including Health (4%), Citizenship and Immigration (9%), and the Canada Mortgage and Housing Corporation (9%). In fact, all departments outside of Justice and Social Programs were reduced by over 10%. In addition, major changes and reductions were made in Employment Insurance.[10]

The enactment of meaningful reductions in nominal spending coupled with fairly stable revenues meant that the government achieved its objective of a balanced budget quickly. As shown in figure 20, it only took two years for the federal government to achieve a balanced budget, which it did in 1997/98. Figure 20 depicts federal budget revenues and total spending as a share of GDP. What is abundantly clear—and critical to understanding the current situation—is that a balanced budget was achieved almost entirely through reductions in spending. Prior to the major tax cuts announced in the 2000 budget,[11] budget revenues were fairly stable, ranging from a low of 17.0% of GDP to 18.2% of GDP.

The achievement of budget surpluses was not short-lived: the federal government was able to manage consistent budget surpluses from 1997/98 to 2007/08. Figure 21a presents the nominal value in billions of dollars of surpluses while figure 21b shows the value of deficits and surpluses as a share of GDP. The surpluses over this period ranged from $1.5 billion in 2004/05 to $19.9 billion in 2000/01. These surpluses were used to reduce the net debt of the country. As a share of the economy, the surpluses ranged from 0.1%

---

10 While Employment Insurance benefits were cut, the government was slow to reduce the contribution rates (payroll tax). The notional "surplus" of employment insurance, which refers to the difference between the revenues collected from the tax and the benefits paid out under the plan, contributed significantly to the elimination of the deficit because both the revenues and spending are included in the general federal budget. This is markedly different from the Canada Pension Plan, since both revenues and spending for CPP are segregated from the government's general budget.

11   Canada, Dep't of Finance, 2000; for a summary of the five-year tax-reduction plan, see chapter four or, on-line, <www.fin.gc.ca/budget00/tax/tax1-eng.asp>.

Table 2: Proposed reductions in departmental spending based on the Program Review

	Spending (billions)		Reductions	
	1994/95	1997/98	$ billions	percent
Natural Resource Sector	4.8	3.3	−1.5	−31%
Agriculture	2.7	1.6	−1.1	−40%
Fisheries and Oceans	0.8	0.6	−0.2	−27%
Natural Resources	1.3	0.6	−0.6	−49%
Environment	0.7	0.5	−0.2	−32%
Transport	2.9	1.4	−1.4	−51%
Industrial, Regional and Scientific Programs	3.8	2.4	−1.4	−38%
Industry	1.3	0.7	−0.6	−43%
Science and Technology Agencies	1.4	1.0	−0.3	−24%
Regional Agencies	1.1	0.6	−0.6	−49%
Justice and Legal Programs	3.3	3.1	−0.2	−5%
Justice	0.8	0.7	−0.1	−8%
Solicitor General	2.5	2.4	−0.1	−4%
Heritage and Cultural Programs	2.9	2.2	−0.7	−23%
Foreign Affairs	4.1	3.3	−0.8	−19%
Foreign Affairs/International Trade	1.5	1.2	−0.3	−17%
International Assistance Envelope	2.6	2.1	−0.5	−21%
Social Programs	13.0	12.0	−1.0	−8%
Citizenship and Immigration	0.7	0.6	−0.1	−9%
Health	1.8	1.7	−0.1	−4%
Human Resources Development	2.5	1.7	−0.9	−35%
Indian Affairs and Northern Development	3.8	4.2	0.4	12%
Canada Mortgage and Housing	2.1	1.9	−0.2	−9%
Veterans Affairs	2.1	1.9	−0.2	−11%
Defence/Emergency Preparedness	11.6	9.9	−1.6	−14%
General Government Services	5.0	4.1	−0.8	−17%
Parliament/Governor General	0.3	0.3	0.0	−10%
Total	51.9	42.1	9.8	19%
Percent of GDP	7%	5%		

Notes: Numbers may not add due to rounding or the exclusion of other relatively minor line items.
Source: Canada, Department of Finance, 1995b.

Figure 20: Federal total revenues and spending (percentage of GDP),
1994/95–2005/06

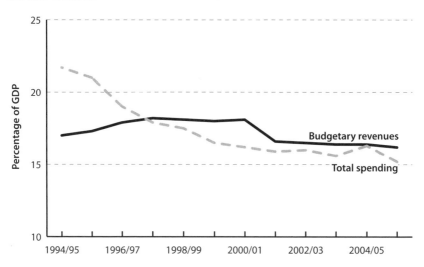

Source: Canada, Department of Finance, 2010c.

in 2004/05 to 1.8% in 2000/01. By both measures, it is clear that the federal
government was able to maintain the balance between spending and revenues
to ensure budget surpluses.[12]

The ongoing surpluses meant that the federal government was able to
reduce the outstanding stock of federal debt. Figures 22a and 22b illustrate
the nominal value of the federal debt as well as federal debt compared to GDP.
The decline in the nominal value of federal debt is stunning: the value of federal
debt (nominal) drops from a high of $562.9 billion in 1996/97 to $457.6 billion
by 2007/08 (figure 22a). Equally as impressive, the federal debt as a share of
GDP declined from 68.4% of GDP in 1995/96 to 29.9% of GDP in 2007/08
(figure 22b). Recall the work by Reinhart and Rogoff (2009) on the deleterious
economic effects of debt accumulation exceeding certain thresholds. The substantial declines in Canadian federal debt, particularly when compared to the

---

12 Interestingly, Paul Martin explained the rationale for government to remain in budget surplus
regardless of economic situation more succinctly and convincingly than almost any economist.
Specifically, Martin argued in his autobiography (2008) that once government ran a deficit (that
is, borrowed money to finance part of its spending) it would quickly become addicted to using
deficits to finance greater spending because it is politically expedient and easier. Such situations
were to be avoided at all costs given the pain of achieving a balanced budget.

Figure 21a: Federal deficit/surplus (nominal $ billions), 1994/95–2007/08

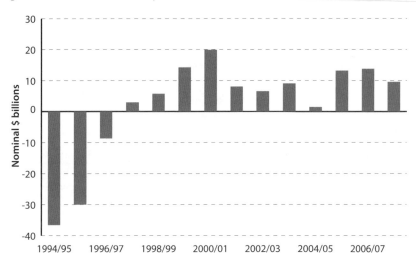

Source: Canada, Department of Finance, 2010c.

Figure 21b: Federal deficit/surplus (percentage of GDP), 1994/95–2007/08

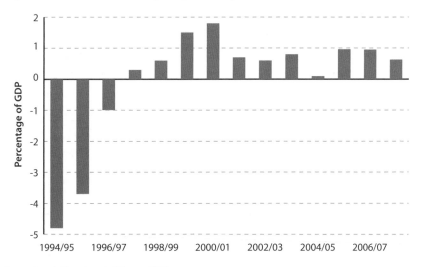

Source: Canada, Department of Finance, 2010c.

Figure 22a: Federal debt (nominal $ billions), 1993/94–2007/08

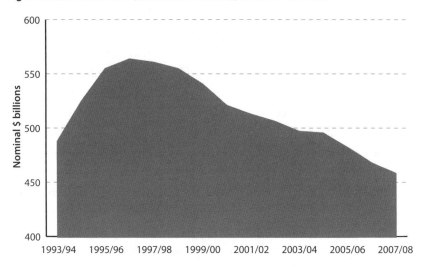

Note: There are several series available for measuring federal debt. The series chosen for this study is accumulated deficits, which measures gross or total debt minus financial and non-financial assets.
Source: Canada, Department of Finance, 2010c.

Figure 22b: Federal debt (percentage of GDP), 1993/94–2007/08

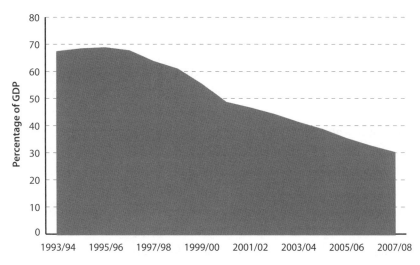

Note: There are several series available for measuring federal debt. The series chosen for this study is accumulated deficits, which measures gross or total debt minus financial and non-financial assets.
Source: Canada, Department of Finance, 2010c.

size of the economy (GDP), had the opposite effect and Canada began enjoying the benefits of lower debt burdens and higher rates of economic growth.

A clear benefit from the return to fiscal balance and the reduction of federal debt was a marked decline in federal interest charges. Figures 23a and 23b illustrate the nominal value of interest charges and interest charges as a share of budget revenues. The nominal value of interest charges for the federal government declined from a high of $49.4 billion in 1995/96 to $29.4 billion in 2009/10. Indeed, the benefits from surpluses and debt reduction in the form of reduced interest payments extended well into the current crisis. This meant that there were more resources available to the federal government for spending and tax relief without increasing total spending since the decline in interest charges, which reduces the wedge between total spending and program spending, allows for greater program spending without increasing total spending. The reduction in the wedge between total resources collected and the amount available to be spent on programs is illustrated in figure 23b, which shows that interest costs as a share of budget revenues declined from a high of 35.2% in 1995/96 to 13.3% in 2008/09. These charges have since begun to rise, though they have not come anywhere near the crisis levels seen in the mid-1990s.

Conclusion

During the 1990s, the federal Liberal Party undertook the deliberate and difficult steps of cutting nominal spending and public-sector employment to solve the deficit and debt problems of the country effectively. They avoided the mistakes of over a decade and a half and took real action. Their approach resulted in meaningful achievements over a short period of time, including balanced budgets, declining debt, and decreasing interest costs. In addition, they established a benchmark process for reviewing, prioritizing, and ultimately reducing government spending through their expenditure review program (1994 and 1995). Their efforts placed Canada in an enviable position around the world as leaders marveled at the fiscal turnaround and its benefits.

Figure 23a: Federal interest charges (nominal $ billions), 1993/94–2009/10

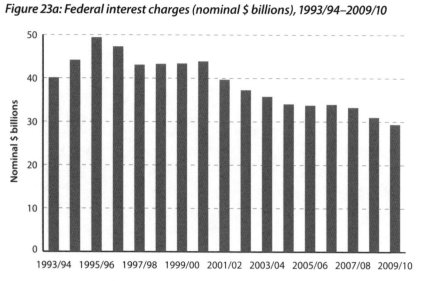

Source: Canada, Department of Finance, 2010c.

Figure 23b: Federal interest charges (percentage of budget revenues), 1993/94–2009/10

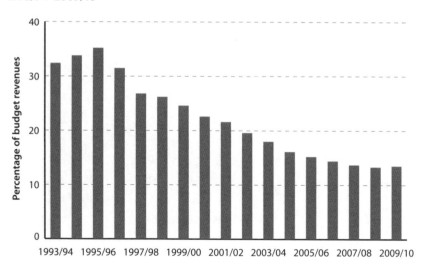

Sources: Canada, Department of Finance, 2010c; calculations by authors.

Chapter 4

Applying federal lessons of the 1990s to today

It should be clear thus far that the federal government struggled with the same fiscal problems during the 1980s and 1990s that confront them today.[1] Unfortunately, the current federal government is relying on the same failed plan. Rather than undertake the difficult task of reducing spending immediately in order to achieve a balanced budget, as the Liberal Party did in 1995, the current government is instead relying on plans for longer-term spending restraint[2] and expected stronger revenue growth to solve its deficit problem.

---

1   This study focuses the comparison between periods on statistics such as government spending, deficits, debt, and interest costs. The purpose for this narrow focus is to show how the parallels between the problems experienced in the 1980s and 1990s compare to the current situation so we can understand how to apply the solutions from the 1990s today. However, there are a host of non-governmental statistics such as interest rates and foreign exchange that also influence economic performance and there are differences among the periods for a number of macro-economic indicators. For instance, governments in the 1980s, 1990s, and 2000s faced very different interest-rate environments. As an example, using the 1-month Treasury Bill interest rate as a gauge of general short-term interest rates: on a monthly basis, the one-month Treasury Bill interest rate ranged from 6.8% to 21.3%, with an average rate of 11.1%, during the 1980s. During the 1990s, the same rate ranged from 2.5% to 13.7%, with an average rate of 6.1%. The rates ranged from 0.1% to 5.5%, with an average rate of 2.9%, during the 2000s (covered up to May 2010) (Source: Statistics Canada, 2010b). Differences in these macro-economic indicators from one period to another, however, do not alter the fundamental conclusion that the budgetary approach of the 1990s was a success while that of the 1980s was a failure.

2   The introduction of the strategic and operating review of spending, which has a goal of identifying and implementing $11 billion in savings over four years beginning in 2012/13 is an important consideration. It would further slow the growth of program spending over the four-year period but would not actually cut spending. In addition, the bulk of the planned cuts will occur in the latter years of the budget plan, 2014/15 and 2015/16.

The same risks observed in the period from 1980 to 1995 are present now: failing to adequately restrain spending, higher debt charges, and lower-than-expected revenue growth.

Figure 24 illustrates the federal government's plans for program spending, based on the last four budgets (2008–2011).[3] Three aspects of figure 24 are worth noting. The first is the nature of the stimulus spending introduced in 2009. The 2008 Budget did not include a stimulus program, as illustrated by the fairly straight line showing planned future program spending. The 2009 budget, which introduced the stimulus spending, deviates from the 2008 spending plan in a limited, temporary manner that reflects stimulus spending: it introduces limited and temporary spending for 2009/10 and 2010/11 and then returns to the pre-stimulus level of spending planned in the 2008 budget. The 2008 and 2009 budgets indicate essentially the same levels of program spending in 2011/12 and 2012/13, after the end of the stimulus program.[4]

Second, note in figure 24 the new higher level of program spending introduced in the *Update* of October 2010. The spending plan announced by the federal government in *Update 2010* deviates permanently from the pre-stimulus spending introduced in the 2009 budget. For example, program spending in the 2009 budget was scheduled to be $235.1 billion in 2011/12 after the stimulus was exhausted. *Update 2010* increases program spending in 2011/12 to $242.7 billion, an increase of 3.2% on top of the stimulus spending. In other words, the federal government has now proposed a permanently higher level of program spending based on the level of program spending established in the stimulus plan of 2009.

Finally, the 2011/12 budget enacted on March 22, 2011[5] reinforced the new higher level of program spending originally proposed in *Update 2010* and, like the *Update*, does not return program spending to its pre-stimulus

---

3 Note that *Update of Economic and Fiscal Projections, October 2010* (Canada, Dep't of Finance, 2010d) was used for the revised 2010 forecasts rather than *Budget 2010* (Canada, Dep't of Finance, 2010a) because the *Update* gives the most up-to-date expectations of the federal government for 2010.

4 The 2008 budget indicates program spending of $235.4 billion and $244.8 billion in 2011/12 and 2012/13 (Canada, Dep't of Finance, 2008). In comparison, the 2009 budget contains program spending of $235.1 billion and $244.5 billion in 2011/12 and 2012/13 (Canada, Dep't of Finance, 2009).

5 The Conservative government tabled a budget on March 22, 2011 that did not pass; this led to a federal election. Upon re-election, the Conservative government passed on June 6 what was essentially the March budget as its 2011 budget (Canada, Dep't of Finance, 2011).

Figure 24: Federal program spending plans (nominal $ billions), 2008–2011 budgets

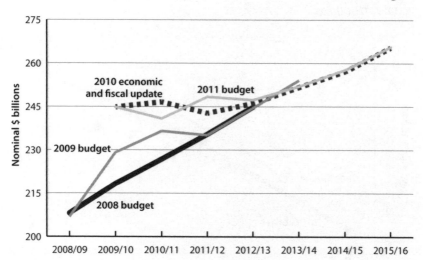

Notes: The figures above do not include spending on interest costs. The program spending from the 2011 Budget does not include the targeted savings of $11 billion (starting in 2012/13) based on the strategic and operating review of spending.
Source: Canada, Department of Finance, 2008, 2009, 2010d, 2011.

level. There are some deviations in program spending between *Update 2010* and the 2011 budget, notably in 2010/11 and 2011/12. However, those differences are largely a matter of timing: the lower program spending recorded in 2010/11 ($5.8 billion) in the 2011 budget is off-set completely by higher spending in 2011/12 ($5.7 billion) than was planned in *Update 2010*. In addition, the 2011/12 budget proposes slightly higher program spending (roughly $2.2 billion) than planned in *Update 2010* for the period from 2012/13 to 2015/16.

The failure to control the growth in spending[6] shown in figure 24 is emblematic of the experience of the 1980s and 1990s. The problems in the government's plan are found to be even worse when revenues are considered. Figure 25 illustrates the budget-revenue expectations of the federal government as outlined in the 2009 and 2010 budgets, *Update 2010*, and the recently passed 2011 budget (Canada, Dep't of Finance, 2009, 2010a, 2010d, 2011). In

---

6 Importantly, though, the federal government has initiated a review of spending based on strategic and operating importance. The goal of the process is to secure $11 billion in savings over four years beginning in 2012/13. For more information, see Canada, Dep't of Finance, 2011: table 5.2.

Figure 25: Revised estimates for federal budget revenues (nominal $ billions), 2009–2011 budgets

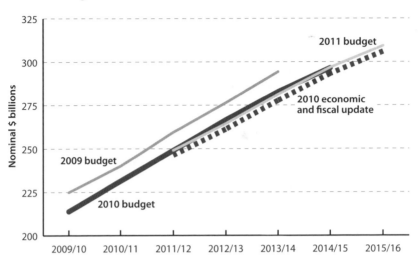

Sources: Canada, Department of Finance, 2009, 2010a, 2010d, 2011.

three of these four budgets—2009 and 2010 budgets, *Update 2010*—, the government had to lower its forecast for future revenues. The revisions are not incidental. For instance, the federal government reduced its four-year revenue forecast by $16.3 billion between the spring 2010 budget and the *Update* of October 2010. Revenue expectations have improved, however, in the forecasts of the recent 2011 budget. Indeed, revenue expectations contained in the 2011 budget, which covers the current fiscal year (2011/12) through to 2015/16, exceed those forecast in *Update 2010* by $16.4 billion.

This experience generally mirrors that of the period from 1980 to 1995. The federal government continuously proved it was unable to control the growth in spending over time and experienced an on-going need to revise its revenue expectations downward. The result of this failure has been discussed at length: continuous deficits that led to increases in federal debt and interest costs. The lesson is that it is prohibitively difficult to achieve balanced budgets by simply restraining spending growth over long periods of time and hoping that revenue growth closes the gap. The insight from the success of the 1995 budget in dealing with the federal government's last deficit and debt problem is that spending cuts implemented over a few years lead to a quick resolution of deficits and sets the stage for a virtuous cycle of fiscal surplus, debt reduction, and declining interest charges. The federal government should heed the lessons of the 1995 budget and move deliberately in its next budget to reduce spending in order to eliminate the deficit in the near term.

Let temporary stimulus spending expire to reduce overall program spending

As its first step in reducing spending and bringing the budget into balance, the federal government should let the provision of 2009/2010 for stimulus spending expire.[7] Stimulus spending is supposed to be temporary and, once funds are exhausted, spending should return to its pre-stimulus level, adjusting for normal growth over time.[8] If spending levels do not return to their pre-stimulus level, which is the case in Canada and many other countries,[9] then the spending was not a "stimulus" but simply more permanent government spending.

Figure 26 illustrates federal program spending beginning in 2002/03 through to 2015/16 (Canada, Dep't of Finance, Canada, 2010d). The effect of the stimulus is self-evident. Program spending spikes from $207.9 billion in 2008/09 to $244.8 billion in 2009/10. However, program spending does not return to its pre-stimulus level but simply grows from the new level established by the stimulus spending, which becomes a new base from which future program spending grows. The stimulus spending was not, therefore, temporary but rather permanent additional spending.

The divergence between the pre-stimulus level of program spending and the new higher base of program spending is illustrated in figure 26. The adjusted program spending line (dashed line) is calculated by increasing the pre-stimulus level of program spending (2008/09) by the annual rate of

---

7 Some may ask why tax increases are not considered. To learn why this is not practicable, see Lammam and Veldhuis, 2010; Taylor, 2011, Jan. 14; Murphy and Clemens, 2010; and Palacios and Harischandra, 2008.

8 "Normal" in this instance could mean growth rates observed over the previous five or 10 years or, more conservatively, growth rates constrained by the rate of economic growth or population growth coupled with inflation.

9 Perhaps the most striking case of a government using stimulus as a rationale to implement significant greater permanent spending is the US federal government in 2008 and 2009. See the Congressional Budget Office's analysis of the US federal government's long-term budget (US-CBO, 2010).

Figure 26: Planned federal program spending compared to lower-growth program spending adjusting for the stimulus (nominal $ billions), 2002/03–2015/16

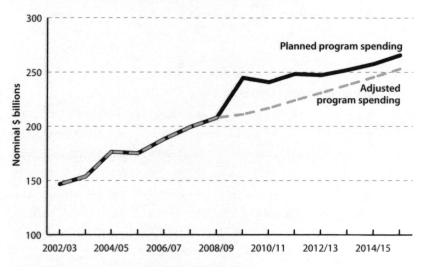

Note: The figures above do not include spending on interest costs.
Sources: Canada, Department of Finance, 2010c, 2011; calculations by authors.

population growth and inflation. The gap between actual planned spending and the spending that may have occurred without the stimulus is $24.5 billion in 2011/12 (see table 4), 75.9% of the expected deficit in that year. This is an important point since it means a substantial portion of the near-term deficit can be eliminated by simply ensuring that temporary stimulus spending be temporary rather than permanent.

Table 3 summarizes the various components of the stimulus spending implemented in 2009/10 and 2010/11. The stimulus plan includes direct spending, tax relief, and additional transfers to individuals, including enhanced Employment Insurance benefits, additional jobs training and placement programs, First Nations initiatives, programs aimed to stimulate the housing sector, infrastructure spending, research and development subsidies, regional subsidies, and new spending on industry, culture, tourism, and the environment.[10]

---

10 For information on the 2009 stimulus plan, see Canada, Dep't of Finance, 2009. Table 1.2 provides a financial summary, tables 3.5, 3.6, 3.7, and 3.8 provide overviews of the various components of the stimulus, and chapter 3 provides both financial and operational details of the stimulus plan.

Table 3: Summary of Stimulus Action in 2009 Federal Budget ($ millions)

	2008/09	2009/10	2010/11
Improving access to financing and strengthening Canada's financial system		162	12
Action to help Canadians and stimulate spending	695	5,880	6,945
Action to stimulate housing construction	530	3,865	1,395
Immediate action to build infrastructure		5,727	5,055
Action to support businesses and corporations	12	2,372	2,121
Plus:			
Capital spending (cash adjustments)		697	685
Loans			
Auto Sector		2,700	
Municipalities for Housing-related Infrastructure		1,000	1,000
Timing of Home Renovation Tax Credit		500	
Total Federal Stimulus		22,742	17,200
Total Stimulus with Leverage		29,298	22,316

Source: Canada, Department of Finance, 2009: table 1.2.

Revised federal fiscal plan

Fortunately, the depth of the current financial problem faced by the federal government is not as severe as that of the 1980s and early 1990s. The overall details of the revised fiscal plan are summarized in table 4 (pp. 48–49). Fiscal 2013/14 was chosen as the target year to achieve a balanced budget based on the two-year time horizon used in 1995.[11] Reductions of $6.3 billion in program spending by 2013/14 are required to bring total spending (program

---

11 It is worth noting that the original paper upon which this chapter is based achieved a balanced budget in 2012/13 because its plan for spending cuts were implemented in 2011/12 and 2012/13. The plan developed in this revised and updated version does not implement cuts in the current year (2011/12) but rather implements the revised plan of program spending in 2012/13 and 2013/14.

and debt servicing) in line with expected revenues. The federal government would have to reduce program spending from the $248.4 billion expected in 2011/12 to $242.1 billion over the following two years in order to achieve a balanced budget in 2013/14.[12] The revised level of program spending for 2013/14 of $242.1 billion is $9.9 billion lower than that planned in the government's 2011 budget (Canada, Dep't of Finance, 2011). It is important to distinguish between the reduction of $6.3 billion in program spending from its current level and the reduction relative to program spending *planned* by the government for that year—$9.9 billion.

The reductions will actually not be as large as presented above because the federal government has already committed itself to identifying $11 billion in savings over four years beginning in 2012/13 through a review of spending based on strategic and operating priorities (figure 2; Canada, Dep't of Finance, 2011: table 5.2). Thus, for example, the reduction in 2012/13 of $3.1 billion (table 4) is only an additional reduction of $2.0 billion beyond current plans.

The total reduction in program spending of $6.3 billion represents a 2.5% reduction in the program spending expected for 2011/12. To put this reduction in context, compare the federal government's calculated stimulus spending of $22.7 billion and $17.2 billion in 2009/10 and 2010/11 and the Liberal Party's reductions in 1995 of nearly 10% over two years.

The reduction in program spending of $6.3 billion (2.5%) by 2013/14 can be achieved a number of ways, such as an across-the-board reduction in spending; or by reviewing and prioritizing spending as was done by the Liberals in 1994 and 1995; or by proportionately reducing stimulus spending that is now included in permanent spending. Below is a categorical summary of the components that were part of the federal stimulus plan of 2009. It is worth examining some of the programs and their costs in order to understand how $6.3 billion in program spending can be eliminated over two years. The following list provides a brief description and price tag (based on 2010/11 cost estimates)[13] for a sample of the programs introduced in the stimulus plan of 2009. The total cost of items in the list is $10.7 billion in 2010/11.

---

12 The suggested program spending of $242.1 billion in 2013/14 needed to balance the budget is $3.9 billion higher than the inflation-adjusted pre-stimulus program spending level needed to account for population growth.

13 The cost estimates were taken from Canada, Dep't of Finance, 2009: chapter 3.

- extension of EI benefits to 50 weeks from 45 weeks ($575 million)[14]
- EI benefits for Canadians in long-term training ($250 million)
- increased training funding for EI generally ($500 million)
- job training for individuals not qualified for EI ($250 million)
- increases to the National Child Benefit Supplement and Canada Child Tax Benefit ($310 million)
- enhancements to the Working Income Tax Benefit ($580 million)
- targeted tax relief for seniors ($340 million)
- enhancing energy efficiency ($150 million)
- first-time homebuyer's tax credit ($180 million)
- funds for renovating and retrofitting social housing ($500 million)
- housing funds for low-income seniors, persons with disabilities, First Nations, and Northern housing ($1.1 billion)
- green infrastructure ($200 million)
- infrastructure stimulus ($2.0 billion)
- contributions and support for Building Canada Fund ($250 million)
- funding for recreational facilities ($250 million)
- on-reserve infrastructure funding ($255 million)
- knowledge initiatives, including infrastructure for universities and colleges, the Canada Foundation for Innovation, and modernizing laboratories ($1.25 billion)
- extending broadband services to rural areas ($100 million)
- federal infrastructure programs ($254 million)
- support for specific sectors of the economy, including forestry, agriculture, slaughterhouses, shipbuilding, and space technologies ($330 million)
- additional support for the Canada Television Fund ($100 million)
- promotion of "Marquee Festivals" ($50 million)
- support for Green Energies ($200 million)
- regional business support and subsidies ($731 million)

---

14 For information on Canada's Employment Insurance system, including the new programs added under the 2009 stimulus, see <www.servicecanada.gc.ca/eng/sc/ei/index.shtml>. For information on the National Child Benefit Supplement, see <www.nationalchildbenefit.ca/eng/home.shtml>; for information on the Canada Child Tax Benefit, see <www.cra-arc.gc.ca/bnfts/cctb/menu-eng.html>. For information on the Working Income Tax Benefit (WITB), see <www.cra-arc.gc.ca/bnfts/wtb/menu-eng.html>. For information on the Building Canada Fund, including details about the Green Infrastructure Fund, infrastructure stimulus fund, and communities components, see <www.buildingcanada-chantierscanada.gc.ca/funprog-progfin/target-viser/bcf-fcc/bcf-fcc-eng.html>.

Table 4: Revised Federal Fiscal Plan, 2011/12 –2015/16

	Budget revenues	Current planned program spending	Debt charges	Total planned spending
2008/09	233.1	207.9	30.7	238.6
2009/10	218.6	244.8	29.4	274.2
2010/11	235.6	240.8	30.9	271.7
2011/12	249.1	248.4	33.0	281.4
2012/13	264.4	247.3	36.5	283.8
2013/14	281.2	252.0	38.6	290.6
2014/15	296.8	257.7	39.4	297.1
2015/16	309.2	265.6	39.4	305.0

Notes: Program spending and debt charges for 2008/09 are taken from the 2009 budget (Canada, Department of Finance, 2009), the remaining data are from the 2011 budget (June) (Canada, Department of Finance, 2011). Total planned spending is simply the addition of planned program spending and debt charges. Revenue figures for 2008/09 to 2009/10 were taken from the 2010 budget (Canada, Department of Finance, 2010a), the remaining figures from the 2011 budget (June) (Canada, Department of Finance, 2011). The program spending from the 2011 Budget does not include the targeted savings of $11 billion (starting in 2012/13) based on the strategic and operating review of spending.

This is just a sampling of the many programs and initiatives included in the 2009 stimulus plan. Some of the programs seem quite distant from a stimulus-type initiative meant to encourage immediate consumption. Indeed, many of the programs seem more like additional permanent spending than they do temporary programs. The nature of these so-called stimulus programs may be part of the explanation why the federal government has not been able to return program spending to pre-stimulus levels.

Many of these programs may be worthy of continuing into the future.[15] This is why the federal government must replicate the review process used in 1994 and 1995 to prioritize federal spending with a concrete goal of reducing

---

15 There are a number of initiatives included in the stimulus plan that should be extended and made permanent. For example, the 2009 budget reduced import tariffs on a range of machinery and equipment goods, making it more economical for Canadian businesses to invest and develop their enterprises in Canada. A summary of the tariff relief program is available in Canada, Dep't of Finance, 2009: 169. Table 3.8 (p. 185) indicates a two-year cost estimate of $169 million, which is a fairly small program that offers enormous economic advantages and benefits. Initiatives like

Budget balance (deficit or surplus)	Adjusted program spending*	Proposed program spending	Adjusted total spending	Adjusted deficit or surplus
−5.5		207.9	238.6	
−55.6		244.8	274.2	
−36.2		240.8	271.7	
−32.3	223.9	248.4	281.4	−32.3
−19.4	231.0	245.3	281.8	−17.4
−9.4	238.2	242.1	280.7	0.5
−0.3	245.5	250.0	289.4	7.4
4.2	253.0	257.6	297.0	12.2

Note: *The Adjusted Program Spending column is calculated by taking 2008/09 pre-stimulus program spending and increasing it annually by the rate of population growth plus inflation.

Sources: Canada, Department of Finance, 2009, 2010a, 2010d, 2011; calculations by authors.

federal program spending by $6.3 billion by 2013/14. The specific plan outlined in table 4 shows program spending being reduced by $3.1 billion in 2012/13 compared to 2011/12 program spending. Program spending is reduced by an additional $3.2 billion in 2013/14.[16] It is assumed, although not dictated, that much of the stimulus spending initiated in 2009 is eliminated or equal amounts of offsetting cuts in other spending are identified.

The revised fiscal plan contained in table 4 results in a budget surplus, albeit minor, beginning in 2013/14. The earlier balanced budget and

this make sense regardless of the country's economic situation and should be extended because they make Canada more attractive for investment and entrepreneurship.

16 There are obviously a number of ways to implement the two-year reduction of $6.3 billion. The plan presented in table 4 distributes cuts evenly between 2012/13 and 2013/14. One could make a case for more aggressive reductions in the first year (2012/13) or for waiting until 2013/14. But, whether the majority of the reductions are made earlier or later, the key is reducing program spending by $6.3 billion by 2013/14 to bring program spending back in line with what would have been the case had pre-stimulus program spending increased based on population growth and inflation.

subsequent surpluses is easily seen in figure 27. The federal government's current fiscal plan calls for the accumulation of debt through deficits of $24.9 billion between 2012/13 and 2015/16, in addition to the expected deficit of $32.3 billion this year (2011/12). The revised fiscal plan results in a small $2.7 billion cumulative surplus over the same period because the budget is balanced sooner than currently anticipated. The quicker return to a balanced budget means less debt accumulation and the availability of surpluses beginning in 2014/15, which allows for higher spending and lower taxes.[17]

Perhaps most importantly, the revised plan shown in figure 27 and table 4 discards the failed principles of the 1980s and early 1990s, which the federal government is relying on today, and builds on the successes of the reform budget of 1995. It calls for reduced program spending largely resulting from the elimination of stimulus spending rather than trying to slow the growth in spending and hoping for strong revenue growth over time. This latter approach failed before, leaving Canada with a large debt and substantial interest payments. The plan offered here heeds the lessons of the reform budget of 1995, which put Canada's federal finances back on track.

Reforming provincial health transfers

There is an opportunity for the federal government to do more than just balance its budget. As it did in the 1990s, the federal government also has an opportunity to reform its relationship with the provinces and, by doing so, provide an incentive for improvement in the delivery of one of Canada's most important social programs. This latter reform is much more controversial than the budget recommendations because it would fundamentally change the relationship between the federal and provincial governments with respect to health care. It is important to understand, however, that like the first recommendation, this reform is also based on our country's experience in the 1990s.

Restructured and reduced provincial transfers—experience from the 1990s

The 1995 budget implemented a major restructuring and reduction in federal transfers to the provinces. Specifically, the budget began a transition away

---

17 The plan outlined in table 4 does not alter the current assumptions regarding debt charges, which would likely be lower given the reduced accumulation of debt.

Figure 27: Federal planned and adjusted total spending and expected budget revenues (nominal $ billions), 2008/09–2015/16

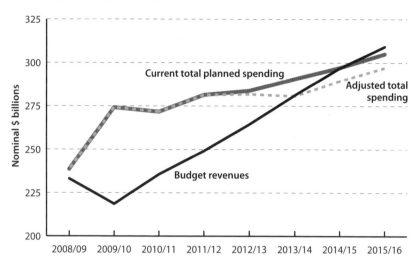

Notes: Program spending and debt charges for 2008/09 are taken from the 2009 Budget (Canada, Department of Finance, 2009, the remaining figures from the 2011 Budget (June) (Canada, Department of Finance, 2011). Revenue figures for 2008/09 to 2009/10 are taken from the 2010 Budget (Canada, Department of Finance, 2010a), the remaining figures from the 2011 Budget (June). The program spending from the 2011 Budget does not include the targeted savings of $11 billion (starting in 2012/13) based on the strategic and operating review of spending.
Sources: Canada, Department of Finance, 2009, 2010a, 2011; calculations by authors.

from federal transfers based on federal-provincial cost-sharing to a block grant. Prior to the 1995 budget, the federal government provided two major transfers[18] to the provinces for programs: the Established Program Financing (EPF) and the Canada Assistance Plan (CAP). EPF was a block transfer to the provinces to support health and post-secondary education spending in the provinces. It was distributed to the provinces regardless of provincial spending in these areas. CAP was a cost-sharing program in which the federal government paid up to half of the amount spent by provincial governments on social services. One of the problems with this approach is the incentives imbedded in it for additional spending, regardless of its efficacy. In this situation, the

---

18 These two transfer programs were specifically related to supporting program spending on health care, post-secondary education, and welfare. They were distinct from the Equalization Program, which is meant to smooth over differences in the provinces' respective abilities to raise own-source revenues. For information on Canada's equalization system, see Clemens and Veldhuis, 2007; and Clemens, Veldhuis, and Palacios, 2007.

provinces could finance an extra dollar of spending on social programs with just 50¢ of provincial revenue as the federal government provided the remaining funds. Critically, this meant that the federal government did not directly control the growth of this federal spending.

The 1995 budget replaced the Canada Assistance Plan (CAP) and the Established Program Financing (EPF) with a new block transfer known as the Canada Social Transfer (renamed the Canada Health and Social Transfer in the 1996 budget) starting in 1996/97.[19] As a result, the negative incentives embedded in the cost-sharing agreement of the Canada Assistance Plan were eliminated. Figure 28 shows the payments under the old EPF/CAP model compared to the revised payments made under the Canada Health and Social Transfer (CHST). The 1995 budget included a reduction in the total amount transferred to the provinces. The EPF and CAP transfers combined were set to fall from $29.3 billion in 1996/97 to $25.1 billion in 1997/98.[20]

The introduction of a single block grant also allowed, and indeed encouraged, the provinces to pursue innovation and improved performance through experimentation based on the increased flexibility and autonomy accorded them by the federal government.[21] Under the earlier cost-sharing arrangements, the federal government controlled standards for social services by connecting the payment of transfers to the provinces to adherence to national standards. This centralized approach and federal regulation meant that provinces were, to a certain extent prohibited, or at least inhibited, from experimenting with alternative delivery models. Indeed, Finance Minister Paul Martin noted in his historic presentation of the 1995 budget that "the restrictions attached by the federal government to transfer payments in areas of clear provincial responsibility should be minimized … they limit innovation … increase administrative costs" (Martin, 1995: 17)."

Canadian welfare reform—decentralization and incentives matter

The CHST reform set off a period of innovation and experimentation in welfare design and delivery across the country. The reduced transfers coupled

---

19 For a history of the Canada Health and Social Transfer, see <www.fin.gc.ca/fedprov/his-eng.asp>.

20 In percentage terms, the reduction in provincial transfers was larger than the reductions applied to federal programs.

21 For a discussion of the reforms in the federal transfers, see Veldhuis and Clemens, 2003.

Figure 28: Transfer payments (nominal $ millions) under EPF/CAP and CHST, 1993/94–2001/02

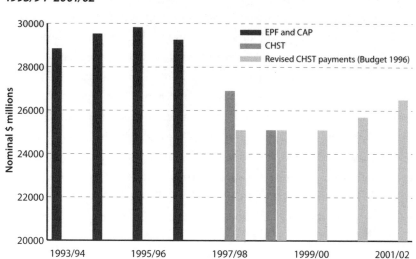

Note: EPF = Established Program Financing; CAP = Canada Assistance Plan; CHST = Canada Health and Social Transfer.
Sources: Canada, Department of Finance, 1994: table 9; Canada, Department of Finance, 1995a, 1995b, 1996.

with greater provincial autonomy and responsibility for welfare and its costs meant that the provinces had the incentive and authority to design and deliver better programs.[22, 23]

Alberta

Alberta was the first province to meaningfully reform welfare. In 1993, Alberta overhauled the administration of the Alberta Family and Social Services Ministry.[24] One of the main avenues of reform was focused on diversion.

---

22 There were a number of common reforms implemented by most, if not all of the provinces. One common feature of reform was a reduction in benefit levels, particularly for single employable people. There was an increasing understanding that, when welfare benefits surpass comparable income available from low-paid work, incentives are created to enter or remain on welfare. Many of the reductions in benefit levels and particularly those for single employable people were aimed at re-establishing a balance between welfare benefits and the income available to workers from low-paid work. For an empirical examination of the relationship between benefit levels and welfare rates during the 1990s, see Emes and Kreptul, 1999.

23 This section is largely based on the summary of provincial welfare reform presented in Crowley, Clemens, and Veldhuis, 2010: chap. 4; it also relies on Schafer, Emes, and Clemens, 2001.

24 For a summary analysis of the reforms implemented in Alberta, see Boessenkool, 1997.

That is, the government shifted the emphasis in the Ministry away from administrative tasks such as determining eligibility and mailing payments to trying proactively to divert people from entering welfare before other possibilities, including employment, were exhausted. The premise of the change was the fact that, once people enter the welfare system, they have a much higher probability of using it again in the future. Thus, people were helped by making sure that every other possible alternative (like finding or staying in work) was exhausted before they could enter the welfare system. The combination of focusing on alternatives to welfare and bringing benefit levels in line with low-paid employment resulted in reductions in welfare dependency and generally improved outcomes for former welfare recipients. One study concluded that almost half of the 172,000 people who left the province's welfare rolls between 1993 and 1996 found full-time employment (Elton, 1997; Canada West Foundation, 1997).

Ontario

Ontario's welfare system had profound problems during the 1990s.[25] In 1994, Ontario had the highest rate of social assistance to population (12.8%) in the country, its spending was increasing at an unsustainable rate, and its benefit levels were encouraging ever higher rates of welfare. The newly elected government in 1995 immediately brought in a number of changes, including reduced benefit rates, an increased focus on diversion to non-welfare alternatives, greater focus on employment, and administrative improvements.

Ontario Works, introduced in 1998, was a formal and fairly broad "workfare" program that was unique in the Canada. The goal of the program was to aid welfare recipients in returning to work. The work requirement was mandatory for all employable adults. The result of the reforms was a reduction in welfare dependency that exceeded the national trends (Finnie, Irvine, and Sceviour, 2005; Roy, 2004; Schafer, Emes, and Clemens, 2001).

British Columbia

British Columbia was one of the last provinces to reform welfare. In 2001, a newly elected Liberal government moved quickly to make wholesale changes

---

25 For a discussion of the problems in Ontario's welfare system prior to reform, see Richards, 1997; for a detailed examination of Ontario's welfare system, see Sabatini, 1996.

to the province's welfare system.[26] Most noticeable was the introduction of a rolling benefit time limit, which mirrored a US reform introduced in 1996: each month a recipient received welfare benefits counted towards a 24-month limit within any 5 year period.[27] The program was effective April 1, 2002.[28] The introduction of a rolling time limit essentially returned the program to being an insurance scheme rather than a source of permanent income.

Across the country

The success of provincial welfare reforms across the country are hard to deny. Welfare dependency was reduced well beyond the cyclical level observed over the previous decade-and-a-half. By 2000, for example, the number of welfare beneficiaries had decreased to slightly over 2 million—6.8% of the population—from a peak of 3.1 million—10.7% of the population (Finnie, Irvine, and Sceviour, 2005; Finnie and Irvine, 2008; Schafer, Emes, and Clemens, 2001). Welfare-related spending also declined and assisted governments across the country in balancing their budgets. Most importantly, the innovation and experimentation encouraged by the reform of federal transfers and regulations meant that provinces were doing a markedly better job of identifying problems and actually helping people back into the labour market.

Applying the lessons of welfare reform to health care

There is broad consensus that one of the short- and long-term issues facing Canada's governments is the delivery and financing of health care. As was the case in 1995, Canada has an opportunity not only to put its financial house in order but also to solve a related social problem, improving health care for Canadians in a financially sustainable manner. The lessons of the success of the 1995 welfare reforms provide a framework for health care reform.[29]

---

26 For a summary and analysis of the reforms enacted in 2001, see Clemens and Schafer, 2002.

27 Reaching the limit for employable individuals resulted in fairly stiff reductions in benefits, to zero in some cases, while more difficult cases like families with children would suffer much smaller reductions in their benefits.

28 As the deadline for the first two-year period in the five-year window of benefit eligibility approached, regulations about penalties and deferrals were extended, which basically nullified the penalties and any real time limit on receipt of benefits (Gabel, Clemens, LeRoy, and Veldhuis, 2003).

29 This approach to deficit reduction and health reform was first discussed while writing *The Canadian Century* (Crowley, Clemens, and Veldhuis, 2010). Credit is due our co-author, Brian Lee Crowley, who was integrally involved in those discussions.

It is first important to outline the challenges facing the federal and provincial governments with respect to health care spending. Figure 29 illustrates the planned transfers from the federal government to the provinces for health care over the next five years. It is fairly clear that health care transfers are growing at a rate well in excess of population and expected inflation as well as real GDP growth. In some years, such as 2012/13, the annual increase in the health-related payment is nearly double the rate of expected GDP growth and almost double the rate of expected population growth and inflation.

The growth in the CHT and CST also outstrips by a wide margin the growth in federal program spending. For example, the average growth in the CHST from 2010/11 through to 2014/15 is expected to be 4.6% while growth in total program spending over the same period is forecast at 1.0%. Therefore, a larger and larger share of program spending at the federal level is being dedicated to health-related transfers to the provinces. Such spending increases are simply not sustainable without either raising taxes or reducing other spending (which is already occurring in relative terms), both of which have their own set of costs that need to be considered.

Canada has already experienced a relative reduction in spending on areas other than health care at the provincial level in order to accommodate the nearly insatiable demand for health spending. Figure 30 illustrates the percentage of total program spending on health care for 1990/91 and 2008/09, the latest year of available data.[30] The total for Canada (that is, all provinces) shows that health spending as a percentage of total program spending has increased from 30.3% in 1990/91 to 36.7% in 2008/09. Every province has experienced an increase in the portion of their budget devoted to health care. Over 40% of total program spending in Nova Scotia and Ontario is already being consumed by health care and a number of other provinces are close to this threshold.

---

30 The series used in figure 30, which is provided by Statistics Canada, is referred to as the Financial Management System (FMS). Statistics Canada adjusts provincially provided numbers in order to accommodate differences in accounting among the provinces and create a consistent and comparable pan-Canadian series of data. Unfortunately, this series has been cancelled and will be replaced by a new series of comparable data in the future. Another important source of information on health care is the Canadian Institute for Health Information (CIHI). See Canadian Institute for Health Information, 2010. Acronyms for provinces in figure 30: BC = British Columbia; AB = Alberta; SK = Saskatchewan; MB = Manitoba; ON = Ontario; QC = Quebec; NB = New Brunswick; NS = Nova Scotia; PE = Prince Edward Island; NL = Newfoundland & Labrador.

Figure 29: Expected growth in CHT and CST payments compared to expected changes in population and CPI, 2009/10–2014/15

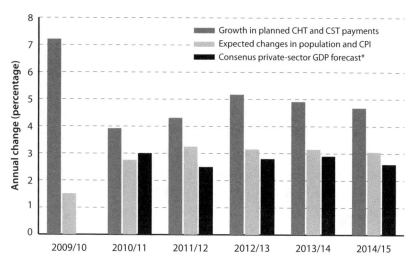

Notes: CHT = Canada Health Transfer; CST = Canada Social Transfer.   * Consensus forecast as of the fall economic and financial update, October 2010. Population was forecast at 10-year average of 1.06% growth rate.
Sources: Canada, Department of Finance, 2010a: table 4.2.5; 2010d: table 2.1; Statistics Canada, 2010a, 2010c; calculations by authors.

Figure 30: Provincial health care spending as a percentage of provincial general spending, 1990/91 and 2008/09

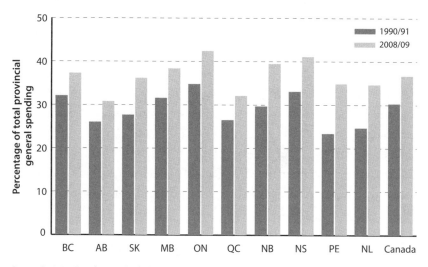

Source: Statistics Canada, 2010d; calculations by authors.

Growth in health spending is also outstripping almost every other area of provincial spending (Kotlikoff and Hagist, 2005). The proportional increase in health spending compared to all other provincial spending coupled with the consistently high rate of annual growth in health care spending means that other categories of provincial spending will continue to be cannibalized in order to finance health care spending unless fundamental changes are introduced.

The other concerning aspect of health care is its quality and timeliness. As was the case with welfare before reform, it appears as if Canadian governments spend substantial resources on health care while Canadians do not enjoy commensurate programs and benefits. Canada's health care system is, on an age-adjusted basis, the developed world's third most expensive[31] after Iceland and the United States. Canada's performance in delivering health care is not commensurate with this comparatively high level of spending. One area where Canada has repeatedly fallen short is waiting times for medical procedures. For example, the total waiting time between referral from a general practitioner and delivery of elective treatment by a specialist was 18.2 weeks in 2010, which constituted an increase from 16.1 weeks in 2009.[32] There were considerable variations among the provinces, ranging from a low of 14.0 weeks in Ontario to 44.4 weeks in Prince Edward Island.

Part of the explanation for Canada's long wait times is a lack of medical professionals and medical technologies. Canada's physician-to-population ratio of 2.2 per 1,000 is one of the lowest (tied for 20th out of 22 countries) in the developed world. Similarly, Canada ranks 17th out of 26 countries for CT scanners (12.7 per million population) and 17th out of 25 countries for MRIs (6.7 per million population) (Rovere and Skinner, 2010). The relatively low access to modern medical technologies also shows up in wait times for these technologies. For instance, in 2010, for Canada as a whole, the wait time for an MRI was 9.8 weeks and 4.5 weeks for an ultrasound (Barua, Rovere, and Skinner, 2010). In addition, much of Canada's medical and diagnostic equipment is outdated and in need of replacement (Esmail and Walker, 2008).

---

31 Tied with Switzerland, where on an age-adjusted basis health expenditures were the same as in Canada in 2005.

32 This calculation is averaged across 12 medical specialties and includes the 10 provinces; see Barua, Rovere, and Skinner, 2010.

Many of these findings are buttressed by *Healthy Canadians*, a report by Canada's ministry of Health that focuses on measuring health performance. For example, the report found that 83.0% of Canadians reported having a regular family doctor in 2007, down from 85.1% in 2003 (Canada, Ministry of Health, 2008: figure 3). However, it is important to recognize that neither 85.1% nor 83.0% are impressive given the universal principle underpinning Canadian health care. Similarly, 25.3% of Canadians in 2007 reported difficulty obtaining immediate care and 17.2% reported difficulty in obtaining routine or ongoing health services, both of which have increased since 2003.[33]

A repeatedly noted barrier to reform and experimentation in health care is the federal government and the monies it transfers to the provinces for health care. These funds are available only to those provinces who abide by the rules, regulations, and federal interpretations of the Canada Health Act.[34] The Act specifically disallows a variety of policies that are being used in other universal health care countries that are able to deliver better care at lower costs. The restrictions include cost sharing and extra billing.

Applying the lessons of the successful welfare reforms introduced in the mid-1990s leads us to a similar opportunity for health care. The federal government should reform CHT payments to reduce provincial dependency on federal transfers while simultaneously providing the provinces more flexibility to experiment with different models of health care delivery within a universal and portable framework. Such an arrangement would allow the provinces to deal honestly with the single largest source of spending and the quickest growing area of spending in provincial budgets.[35]

In exchange for reductions in the planned growth of future CHT payments, the federal government would revise the Canada Health Act to require,

---

33 The figures reported in 2007 represented increases from those in the 2003 report: the percentage reporting difficulty in obtaining immediate care increased from 23.8% in 2003 to 25.3% in 2007 and the percentage reporting difficulty in obtaining routine or ongoing health services increased from 16.4% in 2003 to 17.2% in 2007 (Canada, Ministry of Health, 2008: figure 3).

34 For a detailed explanation of the Canada Health Act, see Canada, Ministry of Health, 2009; for a history of the Canada Health Act, see Orchard and Alsford, 2010.

35 It is important to recognize that, under this approach, roughly 29% of the reduction in program spending by 2012/13 is accomplished through the reduction in the health transfer (CHT) to the provinces.

indeed demand, universality and portability but eliminate the other require-
ments of the CHA. This would afford provinces greater flexibility to experiment and innovate with different health design and delivery models within a
universal and portable framework. To be absolutely clear, this proposal retains
the requirement for universal coverage and portablility. However, it allows
for greater experimentation and testing of different ways in which to deliver
health care services at the provincial level.

It is this experimentation and innovation that will reveal better ways to
provide Canadians with health care commensurate with the resources being
provided.[36] Those reforms might include everything from insurance experimentation to the use of health savings accounts to expanded public coverage.
By allowing the provinces to pursue different methods of delivery, regulation,
and management of health care, we can discover, through experimentation,
better and more cost-effective ways to maintain and improve our nation's
health care system. The key again, however, is to allow experimentation and
innovation within a framework of universal coverage and access.

Conclusion

Two broad reforms have been proposed that would quickly and thoughtfully
eliminate the federal deficit over a two-year period. The first is to ensure that
the temporary stimulus spending introduced in the 2009 budget remains
temporary rather than simply becoming more permanent spending, which
is the current plan. If portions of the stimulus spending are deemed priori-
ties through a review process similar to the one used by the Liberals in 1995,
then spending reductions in other areas should be identified. The second
reform deals with the future of CHT payments and provincial dependence on
such transfers increasing at fairly high rates. Future CHT increases should be
curtailed in exchange for greater flexibility and autonomy for the provinces

---

36 There is another interesting parallel to the health care reforms suggested: Canada's approach
to K-12 education. Canada has no federal involvement in K-12 education and the provinces are
exclusively responsible for its financing, provision, and regulation. Not surprisingly, this has
led to many different approaches to providing primary and secondary education. Interestingly,
Canada spends less and achieves better results than our neighbours to the south, whose system is
increasingly centralized in Washington, DC. For further information on the comparison between
the US and Canadian education, see Izumi and Clemens, 2010 and Izumi, Clemens, and Ou, 2010.

in delivering health care, a proposal based on the successful welfare reforms of the 1990s. The combination of ensuring that stimulus spending is actually temporary rather than simply more permanent spending and the reform of health care transfers and federal regulation offer not only an opportunity to balance the country's financial affairs but to begin solving the various health care problems discussed previously.

Part II

Provincial finances—the provinces forget the lessons of the 1990s

Canada's provincial governments have not escaped the financial and economic costs of the recent recession. Almost all of the provinces* face ongoing deficits, mounting debt, interest costs crowding out real spending on programs, and rising spending pressures. Unfortunately, most of the provinces, like the federal government, have forgotten the lessons of the 1990s and are making the same mistakes made prior to the 1990s reforms. The following chapters examine the provincial experience of the 1990s and relates it to today's challenges and, in doing so, presents a path back to balanced budgets, reduced debt, lower interest costs, sounder overall public finance policy, and renewed economic prosperity.

* "Provinces" is used throughout this paper to refer to provincial governments.

Chapter 5

Provincial finances today and what's the plan?

This chapter examines the basic measures of fiscal policy to assess where the provinces stand today.

Deficits—borrowing to spend

Figure 31 illustrates the deficits and surpluses of the provinces[1] collectively beginning in 2000/01. A deficit simply means that a province (or any other government) spent more than it collected in revenues, requiring it to borrow the difference.[2] In total, the provinces moved from surplus to deficit in 2008/09 as the global recession took hold. The aggregate deficit of the provinces worsened in 2009/10 to 1.8% of GDP. It declined slightly to 1.7% of GDP in 2010/11 and is expected to decline again this fiscal year (2011/12) to 1.5% of GDP.[3]

While figure 31 provides some important general information about the aggregate state of deficits for the provinces, it is important to recognize differences among the individual provinces. Table 5 presents the nominal value of provincial surpluses and deficits for 2009/10 to 2011/12 as well as their values as a share of GDP. The provincial surpluses and deficits are illustrated for the same period in figure 32. Finally, table 6 gives the year in which the

---

1   Total or aggregate data for the provinces includes the territories.

2   Provinces with rainy-day funds or similar accumulated asset reserves can draw down these funds in times of deficit. In a technical sense, they are "dissaving" by drawing down their assets.

3   Forecasts and summary data for 2011/12 are taken from Gulati and Burleton, 2011 (TD Economics).

Figure 31: Total provincial surplus or deficit as a share of GDP, 2000/01–2011/12

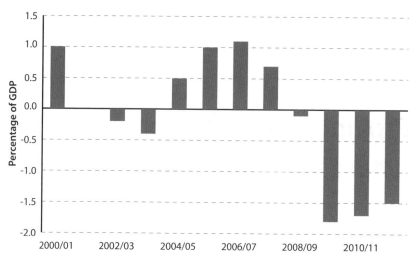

Notes: The totals include surplus and deficit figures for the Canadian territories. Data up to 2009/10 is taken from the Department of Finances' Fiscal Reference Tables; the forecasts for 2010/11 and 2011/12 are taken from TD Economics' Government Budget Balances and Net Debt.
Source: Canada, Department of Finance, 2010c: table 31; TD Economics, 2011.

each provincial government is expected to attain a balanced budget, based on their most recent budget. Combined these measures provide a broad assessment of the deficit situations present in each province.

Several aspects of provincial deficits and surpluses are illuminated in table 5 and figure 32. First, Ontario had the largest deficit both in nominal terms and as a share of the economy in all three years. Second, New Brunswick has one of the larger persistent deficits compared to the size of the provincial economy. Third, Nova Scotia showed improvement in 2010/11 but slipped back into deficit in 2011/12. Finally, Saskatchewan was the only province to record a balanced or surplus budget over the entire period. Using the data in table 5 and figure 32, we can roughly categorize the provinces based on the severity of their current deficits.[4] Such rough categorization allows us to

---

4 For information on provincial budgets, see Alberta, Department of Finance and Enterprise, 2011; British Columbia, Ministry of Finance, 2011a, 2011b; Manitoba, Department of Finance, 2011; New Brunswick, Department of Finance, 2011a, 2011b; Newfoundland & Labrador, Department of Finance, 2011; Nova Scotia, Department of Finance, 2011; Ontario, Ministry of Finance, 2011; Saskatchewan, Ministry of Finance, 2011; Prince Edward Island, Department of Finance and Municipal Affairs, 2011; Quebec, Department of Finance, 2011.

Table 5: Deficits and surpluses of the provincial governments

	$millions (nominal)			As a share of GDP (%)		
	2009/10	2010/11	2011/12	2009/10	2010/11	2011/12
British Columbia	−1,779	−1,265	−925	−0.9	−0.6	−0.4
Alberta	−1,032	−4,821	−3,405	−0.4	−1.8	−1.2
Saskatchewan	425	20	383	0.8	0.0	0.6
Manitoba	−201	−467	−438	−0.4	−0.8	−0.6
Ontario	−19,262	−16,700	−16,300	−3.3	−2.7	−2.6
Quebec	−3,174	−4,200	−3,797	−1	−1.3	−1.2
New Brunswick	−738	−740	−449	−2.7	−2.6	−1.5
Nova Scotia	−242	447	−390	−0.7	1.2	−1.0
Prince Edward Island	−120	−54	−42	−2.5	−1.1	−0.8
Newfoundland & Labrador	−295	485	59	−1.2	1.6	0.2

Note: Figures are based on government forecasts and estimates.
Sources: Gulati and Burleton, 2011; TD Economics, 2011.

Figure 32: Provincial surplus or deficit (percentage of GDP), by province, 2009/10, 2010/11, and 2011/12

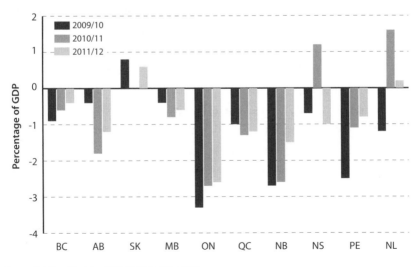

Source: Gulati and Burleton, 2011; TD Economics, 2011.

Table 6: Expected Year of Deficit Elimination

Saskatchewan	N/A	Prince Edward Island	2014/15
		Manitoba	2014/15
British Columbia	2013/14	New Brunswick*	2014/15
Alberta	2013/14	Newfoundland & Labrador*	2014/15
Nova Scotia	2013/14	Federal Government	2014/15
Quebec	2013/14	Ontario	2017/18

Note: Please note that the TD Bank Report from which this table was copied categorized NB and NL as N/A based on their surpluses (2010/11). The authors chose to include the 2014/15 date of deficit elimination for both provinces based on their recent budgets. To obtain the New Brunswick budget for 2011/12, see <http://www.gnb.ca/0024/index-e.asp>; to obtain the 2011/12 budget for Newfoundland & Labrador, see <http://www.budget.gov.nl.ca/budget2011/default.htm>.
Sources: Gulati and Burleton, 2011; New Brunswick, Department of Finance, 2011; Newfoundland & Labrador, Department of Finance, 2011.

understand the varying imperatives for solving each province's fiscal imbalance. Saskatchewan stands alone in the first category, since it is the only province that operated in balance or surplus over the three years examined, and forecasts balanced budgets for the foreseeable future.

The second group of provinces includes those making clear progress towards returning to fiscal balance but currently still have a fairly small deficit as a share of the economy. This group includes British Columbia, Manitoba, and Prince Edward Island. British Columbia has more than halved the size of its deficit since 2009/10 as a share of the economy while Prince Edward Island reduced its deficit as a share of GDP by more than 75%. Manitoba's deficit worsened in 2010/11 but is expected to improve during the course of this year. In addition, Manitoba's expected budget deficit of 0.6% for 2011/12 is comparatively small. The fact that only four of the ten provinces fit into the category of being in surplus or making clear progress towards returning to surplus is telling of the current fiscal situation in the provinces.

The third category includes provinces making limited progress in 2011/12 but expect to return to a balanced budget by 2013/14. This group includes Alberta and Quebec. Both provinces are expected to record deficits of 1.2% of GDP in 2011/12 but experience improvements over the next two years.

The fourth category, which is also the largest, comprises provinces where there is inconsistent performance (Newfoundland & Labrador; Nova Scotia) or a worrying lack of improvement (Ontario; New Brunswick). The province of Newfoundland & Labrador, while in surplus last year and expected to be in surplus in 2011/12 forecasts deficits in both 2012/13 and 2013/14: 1.5% of GDP next year, then declining to 0.9% of GDP before turning into a small surplus in 2014/15. Similarly, Nova Scotia expects to be in a deficit during 2011/12 as well as the following two years before returning to a small surplus in 2014/15 (table 6). New Brunswick has made some improvement in its fiscal position, reducing its deficit from 2.7% in 2009/10 to 1.5% in 2011/12. However, in 2011/12, New Brunswick will incur one of the highest deficits in the country: 1.5% as a share of the economy. New Brunswick has committed itself to achieving a balanced budget in 2014/15 but has provided very little detail about how it will achieve this goal.[5] Ontario is perhaps the most worrying of all the provinces when it comes to deficits. Its current deficit of $16.3 billion is almost twice as much as the other nine provinces combined (table 5). Its deficit for 2011/12 of 2.6% is down only slightly from the previous year (2.7%). More worrying is that Ontario does not expect to return to balance until 2017/18 (table 6), which means it will accumulate debt between now and then.

Another way to understand the relative deficits of each of the provinces is to compare the provincial shares of national GDP with the provincial shares of the combined total provincial deficit. Figure 33 illustrates the provincial share of the total deficit for 2009/10 as well as each provinces' share of national GDP. There are several points worth noting from the data presented in figure 33. First, almost the entire cumulative provincial deficit of the ten provinces is held by Ontario (72.7%) and Quebec (12.0%). Tellingly, there are only two provinces where their share of the total provincial deficit is larger than their share of GDP: Ontario and New Brunswick. The difference in New Brunswick is fairly small: 1.8% of GDP compared to 2.8% of the total (aggregate) provincial deficit. Ontario, on the other hand, has 37.9% of total GDP but almost three-quarters (72.7%) of the total provincial deficit.

In reviewing the data presented for the provinces with respect to their individual deficits, Ontario stands alone in terms of the severity of its deficit, which is both large and persistent. There is also cause for concern for a number of other provinces such as Newfoundland & Labrador, Nova Scotia, and New Brunswick and most of the remaining provinces should proceed cautiously. The only province that seems clear of worry regarding deficits is Saskatchewan.

---

5 For a commentary and summary of New Brunswick's 2011/12 budget, see Gulati, 2011b.

Figure 33: Provincial governments' shares of the 2009/10 deficit compared with their share of total GDP

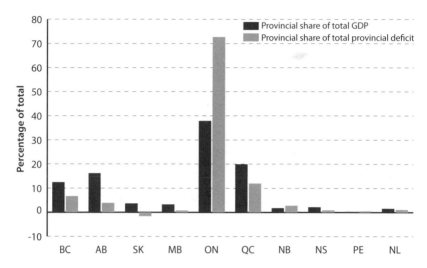

Note: Total does not add to 100 because Territories are not included.
Source: TD Economics, 2011; Statistics Canada, 2010e.

Debt—accumulation of deficits

Since they have deficits, the provinces are, not surprisingly, accumulating debt. Figure 34 illustrates the nominal value of all provincial debt beginning in 2000/01 as well as its value as a share of the economy. The nominal value of total provincial debt has been increasing each year since 2000/01 with the exception of 2002/03: total provincial debt (nominal) stood at $284.0 billion in 2000/01 and is expected to reach $486.8 billion in 2011/12 (Gulati and Burleton, 2011). Figure 34 also includes a measure of total provincial debt as a share of the economy. The rate of increase in the nominal value of provincial debt discussed above, which began increasing at a higher rate in 2007/08 as the effects of the recession began to surface meant that debt began to increase as a share of the economy. Total provincial debt increased from a low of 20.6% in 2007/08 to 28.4% forecast for 2011/12 (Gulati and Burleton, 2011). This means the burden of debt is increasing relative to the size of the economy.[6]

---

6   This is a particular concern given that rising debt levels impose large economic costs on jurisdictions once they reach a certain threshold. Recent work by Reinhart and Rogoff (2009) confirms this effect. See also <http://reinhartandrogoff.com/> for links to, and summaries of, related research.

Figure 34: Measures of total provincial government debt, 2000/01–2011/12

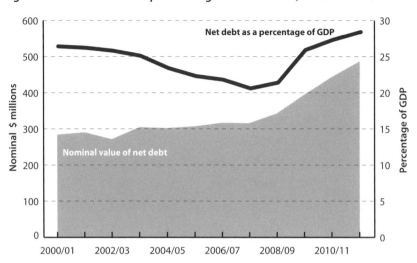

Notes: Net debt is gross debt (total) minus financial assets. Totals include debt figures for the Canadian territories.
Sources: TD Economics, 2011; Statistics Canada, 2010e.

Table 7 contains the nominal value of provincial debt and debt compared to the size of the economy beginning in 2009/10 through to the expectation for the current year (2011/12) as well as the percentage change over the
three year period. Table 7 shows some worrying trends in provincial debt.
First, all of the provinces—even Saskatchewan, which is running surpluses—
are accumulating debt.[7] The increases (nominal) in provincial debt over the
three years from 2009/10 to 2011/12 range from 2.8% in Saskatchewan to
28.6% in British Columbia. Second, Ontario's debt represents almost half
of the total provincial debt in the country. Third, Alberta's negative figures
for debt in the table reflect the fact that the province has more assets than
debt and is in a net asset position rather than a net debt position. However,
the province has drawn down nearly $14 billion in assets since 2009/10. In
other words, Alberta's current revenues compared to current spending since
2009/10 have been short (in deficit) by nearly $14 billion.

---

7   In addition to accumulating debt through deficits, provinces can accumulate debt through
capital borrowing to finance capital expenditures. Depending on the accounting system used in
each province, some of these capital expenditures may appear outside of the operating budget.

Table 7: Provincial government debt by province

	$billions (nominal)				As a share of GDP (%)			
	2009/10	2010/11	2011/12	Change	2009/10	2010/11	2011/12	Change
BC	28.0	31.5	36.0	28.6%	14.7	15.6	17.1	16.3%
AB*	−23.7	−14.0	−10.0	−57.8%	−9.6	−5.2	−3.4	−64.6%
SK	3.6	3.6	3.7	2.8%	6.4	6.1	5.7	−10.9%
MB	11.8	13.2	14.8	25.4%	23.1	24.7	26.2	13.4%
ON	193.6	217.3	241.5	24.7%	33.5	35.6	37.8	12.8%
QC	150.1	159.0	166.1	10.7%	49.4	50.1	50.4	2.0%
NB	8.4	9.6	10.2	21.4%	30.4	33.6	34.2	12.5%
NS	13.3	13.1	13.7	3.0%	38.9	36.3	36.6	−5.9%
PE	1.6	1.8	1.9	18.8%	33.4	35.2	36.0	7.8%
NL	8.2	8.2	8.7	6.1%	32.9	27.7	26.7	−18.8%

Note: Figures are based on government forecasts and estimates.   * Alberta's negative figures for debt reflect the fact that the province has more assets than debt and is in a net asset position rather than a net debt position. Source: Gulati and Burleton, 2011.

Table 7 also contains data about the provinces' debt as a share of the provincial economy. Quebec maintains the highest debt level as a percentage of GDP at 50.4% and is perilously close to the threshold of 90% identified by research as a threshold for debt-to-GDP ratios. Research has demonstrated that when jurisdictions' public debt reaches or exceeds 90% of the economy (GDP), economic costs begin to be imposed on the jurisdiction in the form of slower economic growth.[8] Quebec's ratio of debt to GDP is fairly close to 90% when one considers that the federal government's debt-to-GDP ratio is 34.3% (2011/12) and the debt shown for Quebec does not include local and other debt in the province (Gulati and Burleton, 2011). Ontario (37.8%), Nova Scotia (36.6%), Prince Edward Island (36.0%), and New Brunswick (34.2%) follow Quebec in terms of debt compared to GDP. Saskatchewan maintains the lowest debt burden relative to the economy (5.7%) among the nine provinces with net debt (recall that Alberta has more assets than it does debt, resulting in net assets rather than net debt).

---

8   See footnote 6 for information on critical research into the economic costs of debt.

It's also worth noting the trends calculated in table 7 for debt as a share of the economy. Three provinces experienced a decline in the ratio of their provincial debt compared to their economy: Saskatchewan, Nova Scotia, and Newfoundland & Labrador. Six provinces experienced an increase in the ratio of provincial debt to the provincial economy, ranging from 2.0% in Quebec to 16.3% in British Columbia. Finally, Alberta experienced a large drop in the value of its net assets compared to the economy: a decline of nearly 65%.

Figure 35 compares each province's share of total provincial debt against its share of GDP. Figure 35 illustrates the serious debt situations facing both Ontario and Quebec. In 2009/10, Ontario represented 37.9% of the economy but had 49.0% of the total stock of provincial debt. Similarly, Quebec represented 19.9% of the total economy but had 38.0% of the total provincial debt. Both of these debt statistics worsen if adjustment is made in the anaylsis for Alberta's positive position of having more assets than debt.

There is another factor to consider in figure 35: east-west polarity. The four western provinces all have debt levels relative to the total that are less than their respective shares of total GDP. Ontario, Quebec, and the four Atlantic provinces, on the other hand, all have relative debt positions higher than their respective shares of the national economy. Quebec is clearly struggling with very serious debt levels and, if this is not contained quickly by balancing the provincial budget and ceasing to borrow for capital spending, it will inevitably impose large and sustained economic costs on the province, particularly in the form of slower economic growth. Other provinces, principally Ontario and the Atlantic provinces save for Newfoundland & Labrador are also struggling with provincial debt.

The increase in British Columbia's provincial debt should also be noted with caution, since most of the increase is taking place with respect to capital expenditures rather than within the operating budget as part of the province's long-term infrastructure investment plan.[9] Alberta, although

---

9   The main source of increase in British Columbia's debt is not the accumulation of deficits or direct debt but rather spending on infrastructure, which appears in the financial statements as taxpayer-supported debt. This category of provincial debt is forecast to reach $36.8 billion in 2011/12, an increase of $3.4 billion or 10.3%. Taxpayer-supported debt includes capital spending on hospitals, schools, post-secondary facilities, transit, and roads. Another category of debt that is also increasing is self-supported debt, which includes debt accumulated by the provincial

Figure 35: Provincial governments' shares of net debt compared with their share of total GDP, 2009

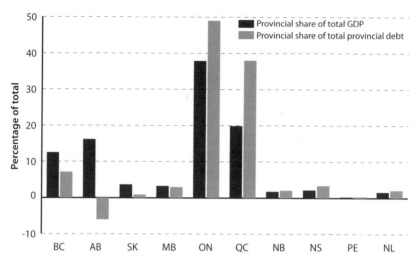

Notes: Net debt is gross debt (total) minus financial assets. The negative value for Alberta's share of total provincial debt reflects the fact that the province holds more assets than provincial debt, resulting in a net surplus position for the province. Total does not add to 100 because the Territories are not included.
Source: TD Economics, 2011; Statistics Canada, 2010e.

at this time it has no net provincial debt, is aggressively drawing down its assets due to over-spending, which must be curtailed in order to stabilize the province's finances.[10]

---

utilities company that provides electrical generation, transmission, and distribution. This category of debt is scheduled to increase to $16.3 billion in 2011/12, an increase of $2.5 billion or 18.4%. Critically, the province expects infrastructure and capital spending more broadly to return to a more historical level beginning next year (British Columbia, Ministry of Finance, 2011b: table 1.1, p. 5; table 1.12, p. 25).

10 The reduction in assets by the Alberta Government is actually quite alarming. For example, the net-assets position of the government, the difference between financial and capital assets compared to debt or liabilities, has declined from $53.6 billion in 2007/08 to an expected $42.3 billion in 2011/12, a decline of 21.0% (Alberta, Ministry of Finance, 2011: Historical Fiscal Summary Table, p. 88). Perhaps more telling of the province's drawdown in assets is the near exhaustion of the province's Sustainability Fund. Since peaking in 2009/10 at nearly $15.0 billion, the fund has declined to an expected $5.3 billion in 2011/12, a decrease of 64.7% in two years. It is expected to decline further to $1.7 billion by 2013/14, a decrease of 88.6% (Alberta, Ministry of Finance, 2011: Sustainability Fund Table, p. 67; Historical Fiscal Summary Table, p. 88). Fiscal Plan Tables are available at <www.finance.alberta.ca/publications/budget/budget2011/fiscal-plan-tables.pdf>.

Interest costs—the price of debt

The provinces' standing with respect to debt levels is also illustrated in the burden of interest or debt charges each carries to maintain their debt levels. Interest costs create a wedge between what a province collects in revenues and what it is able to actually spend on programs and transfers. Figure 36 shows the share of revenues that each province must allocate to pay the debt charges on their outstanding debt as of 2009/10. This figure does not include any retiring of provincial debt but only the borrowing cost of debt in the form of interest charges.

The same east-west dichotomy in figure 35 is evident in figure 36 as well. The four western provinces have the lowest burden of interest charges, which range from 5.9% of revenues in Manitoba to 0.6% of revenues in Alberta. Newfoundland & Labrador recorded the highest burden of interest costs at 13.2% of revenues.

Tackling the deficit—comparing provincial plans

Thus far the analysis has been restricted to the current state of provincial finances with attention focused on fiscal balance (deficits), debt, and interest costs. There is a critical final component to consider in evaluating the state of fiscal policies across the provinces: how each province plans to tackle the deficit and debt problems facing them today. As discussed previously, each province except for Saskatchewan is facing some type of fiscal challenge relating to deficits, increasing debt, and interest costs. Table 8 presents summary data of the plans each province has presented to solve their deficit and debt problems. The period covered for each province runs from the current year (2011/12) to the year in which the government expects to have a balanced or surplus budget. There are no data for Saskatchewan in the table since it is currently in surplus and expects to remain in surplus for the foreseeable future. New Brunswick and Prince Edward Island were excluded from table 8 as their 2011/12 budgets lacked the information required for the calculations. Both provinces failed to present revenue and spending expectations beyond the current year of operations (2011/12).

Five of the seven provinces shown in table 8—British Columbia, Alberta, Manitoba, Ontario, and Quebec—rely on a combination of robust

Figure 36: Provincial government debt charges as a percentage of total revenues, 2009/10

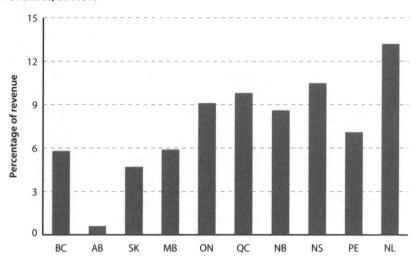

Note: Total revenues include both own-source revenues for the province and transfers from the federal government.
Source: Canada, Department of Finance, 2010c: table 30; calculations by the authors.

Table 8: Growth rates in revenues and spending for deficit provinces (percent)

	Revenues	Program spending	Number of years with spending reductions	Year when balanced budget expected	Number of years to balance[1]
British Columbia	3.4	1.5	0	2013/14	3
Alberta	7.3	1.5	0	2013/14	3
Saskatchewan[2]	N/A	N/A	N/A	N/A	N/A
Manitoba	3.2	1.8	0	2014/15	4
Ontario	4.3	1.4	0	2017/18	7
Quebec	4.9	1.9	0	2013/14	3
New Brunswick[3]	N/A	N/A	N/A	2014/15	4
Nova Scotia	0.5	1.8	1	2013/14	3
Prince Edward Island[3]	N/A	N/A	N/A	2014/15	4
Newfoundland & Labrador	0.4	1.8	1	2014/15	4

Notes: The averages presented were calculated over the period required in each province to achieve a balanced budget. [1] The number of years to balance the budget runs from 2011/12 to the year of balance. [2] Saskatchewan was in a surplus positions in 2011/12 and excluded from the analysis. [3] New Brunswick and Prince Edward Island were excluded from the analysis as their 2011/12 budgets lacked the information required for the calculations. Sources: Gulati and Burleton, 2011; federal and provincial budgets (various); calculations by the authors.

revenue growth coupled with constrained growth in program spending to reach a balanced budget. In other words, these five provinces prefer to try to slow the rate of increase in spending while hoping for revenues to catch up in order to balance their budget.[11] The gap between the expectations for revenue growth in these five provinces compared to planned increases in program spending is shown in figure 37. Put simply, these five provinces are relying on a strong rebound in revenues coupled with slower growth in spending to achieve a balanced budget. Only Nova Scotia appears to rely on near-term spending cuts with normal, even conservative expectations for revenue growth in the future and constrained spending growth.[12] The annual average revenue growth for the provinces shown in figure 37 ranges from 3.2% in Manitoba to 7.3% in Alberta over the period covered. Program spending, on the other hand, ranges from 1.4% in Ontario to 1.9% in Quebec. Clearly each of the five provinces relies on slowing the growth in program spending coupled with a robust rebound in revenues to balance their financial affairs.

Another way to examine the data in table 8 is to compare the number of budgets required by the provinces to achieve a balanced budget against the numbers of years in which a decline in program spending is expected. Altogether, there are 35 budgets required by the seven provinces[13] to achieve

---

11 Newfoundland & Labrador also generally relies on this approach although this is less clear based on the numbers in table 8. The figures contained in table 8 indicate that program spending will grow, on average, at a higher rate than revenues over the period covered. However, the budget plan presented by the provincial government is generally in line with those offered by the five provinces, relying on slowing spending growth coupled with strong revenue collections. The numbers for Newfoundland & Labrador look otherwise because of the effect of one year in which there is a large change. For example, program spending in the province is expected to increase on average by 1.8%. However, the province plans a 4.9% increase in spending this year, which is accounted for in the lower annual average by including a 1.0% decline in program spending scheduled for 2014/15. Similarly, revenues in Newfoundland & Labrador are expected to decline by 5.8% next year but rebound by 4.9% and 4.4% in 2013/14 and 2014/15, allowing the province to achieve a balanced budget (Newfoundland & Labrador, Dep't of Finance, 2011).

12 The 2011/12 budget for Nova Scotia relied on $3-$4 in spending reductions for every $1 increase from revenues to achieve a balanced budget in 2013/14. The program spending cuts included a reduction in the public sector of 10%, freezing of transfers to district health authorities, and reductions in grants to school boards and universities. For a summary of, and commentary on, Nova Scotia's budget for 2011/12, see Gulati, 2011a.

13 The seven provinces in table 8 plus Nova Scotia and Newfoundland & Labrador.

Figure 37: Annual average growth in provincial revenue and program spending, 2011/12 to year when balanced budget or surplus expected

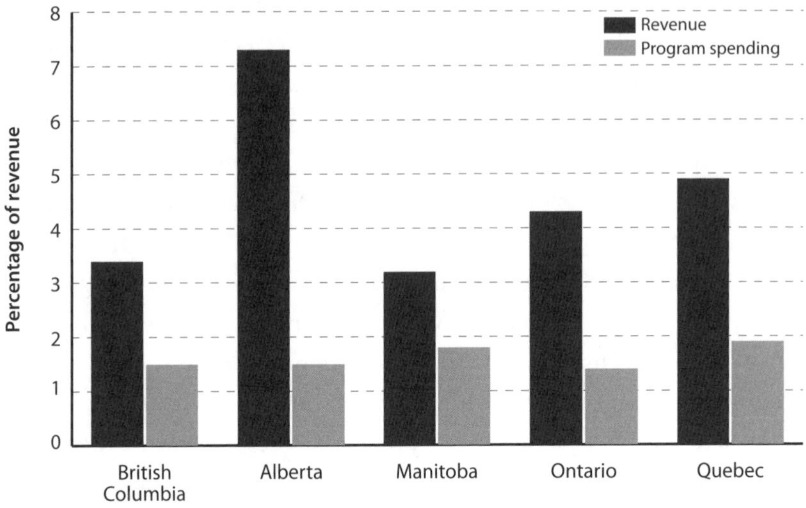

Notes: Saskatchewan was in a surplus position in 2011/12 and excluded from the analysis. New Brunswick and Prince Edward Island were excluded as they did not provide sufficient information in their 2011/12 budgets to allow for the calculations required. Nova Scotia and Newfoundland & Labrador were excluded due to variances in the growth of their revenue and program spending that made the calculations misleading for the period in question. Source: Gulati and Burleton, 2011; federal and provincial budgets (various); calculations by the authors.

a balanced budget. This ranges from three years in several provinces to seven years in Ontario. In only two of the 35 budgets included in this period are program spending by the provinces actually scheduled to decline. Interestingly, the two years of cuts are proposed by Nova Scotia—a 2.4% reduction in program spending in 2012/13—and Newfoundland & Labrador—a 1.0% cut in 2014/15.

All the provinces for which we have data, except Nova Scotia, rely on slowing the growth in program spending coupled with a rebound in revenues. There are a number of inherent risks in this strategy. First, revenues may not materialize as expected due to slower economic growth or, for those provinces with large natural resources, lower commodity prices than forecast. Second, program spending may increase faster than anticipated for a number of reasons such as natural disasters, political pressure, and higher entitlement spending than expected. Third, interest costs, which are not negotiable, may also turn out to be higher than expected. Put simply, relying on stronger revenue growth in the future is a passive approach to solving current fiscal problems.

Conclusion

All of the provinces except for Saskatchewan are in a deficit and accumulating debt. There is some meaningful variance among the provinces in terms of the size and manageability of the deficits and debt, as well as the interest costs associated with provincial debt. The Western provinces seem to be in better positions than either Central Canada or Atlantic Canada. The situations in Ontario, Quebec, and New Brunswick are of particular concern.

Chapter 6

Déjà vu—the provinces have been here before

As they do today, the provinces in the 1980s and early 1990s struggled with deficits, growing debt, and interest costs. This chapter summarizes and analyzes the situation faced by the provinces and their response to it during this period. On a consolidated or total basis, the provinces operated in deficit throughout the period from 1986/87 to 1995/96.[1] Figure 38 presents the total annual deficit of all the provinces as a share of the economy (GDP). The annual deficits ranged from a low of 0.9% of GDP (1988/89) to 3.5% of GDP (1992/93). Although not as large as the federal deficits during this period, the ongoing, continuous nature of the deficits was a justified source of concern. In other words, one concern about the provincial deficits was that the provinces could not seem to balance their budgets regardless of the state of the economy. A structural or permanent deficit seemed to exist with the provinces.

As one might expect, there were important differences between the fiscal positions of the various provinces. Figure 39 illustrates the annual deficit for each of the provinces in 1992/93, the height of the provincial deficit during this period. The annual deficit ranged from a low of 1.7% of GDP in British Columbia to 4.4% of GDP in Alberta, with Ontario close to Alberta at 4.3% of GDP.

---

1   The year 1986/87 was selected as a beginning based on the availability of public accounts (PA) data. A different series of PA data is available prior to 1986/87 but is not directly comparable. For longer historical analysis, see Statistics Canada, National Economic Accounts at <http://www.statcan.gc.ca/nea-cen/index-eng.htm>.

Figure 38: Total provincial surplus or deficit as a share of GDP, 1986/87–1995/96

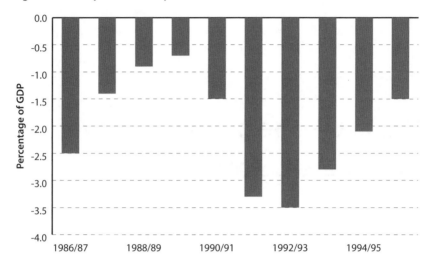

Notes: The totals include surplus and deficit figures for the Canadian territories.

Source: Canada, Department of Finance, 2010c: table 31.

Figure 39: Provincial government surplus or deficit as a share of GDP, 1992/93

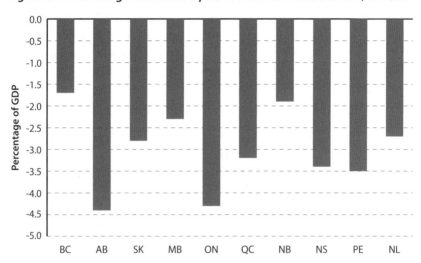

Source: Gulati and Burleton, 2011.

The provinces collectively experienced a marked increase in their debt. Figure 40 presents the total stock of provincial debt as a percentage of GDP. There are two debt series presented in figure 40. The first series, illustrated by the area graph begins in 1980 and continues to 1995. It is based on Statistics Canada's *National Economic Accounts* (Statistics Canada, 2008). According to this data, total provincial debt increased from 5.5% of GDP in 1980 to 27.6% of GDP in 1995. The second data series, shown as a line graph, is based on Public Accounts data (Gulati and Burleton, 2011) and is readily comparable to the other data used in this study. This data series begins in 1986/87 and links directly to the fiscal years of government rather than the calendar years used in the *National Economic Accounts*. According to the Public Accounts data, provincial debt rose from 15.2% in 1986/87 to 27.7% in 1995/96. Critically, the two series are very close with one another and show the same trend over the period examined.

The increasing debt of the provinces meant more and more resources were being devoted to interest costs. Figure 41 illustrates the share of budget revenues allocated to interest costs between 1986/87 and 1995/96. Provincial interest costs as a share of budget revenues increased from a little over 10% in 1986/87 to 14.1% in 1995/96. Put differently, in 1995/96 over $1 out of every $6.50 collected in revenues were spent on interest costs rather than programs and services.

Conclusion

The parallels between the situations faced today and then are striking. Governments in both periods faced deficits and increasing debt coupled with interest costs that curtailed spending on real programs and services. For years, the various provincial governments attempted to slow the growth in program spending and wait for revenues to rebound strongly enough to close the gap between spending and resources. As the data illustrates, the results were on-going deficits, mounting debt, and increasing interest costs. Fortunately, the 1990s were a period of reform and a different approach to solving the deficit and debt problems that plagued the provinces. The success of the 1990s and the lessons available from that period are critical to today and solving our present problems.

Figure 40: Total provincial government debt as share of GDP, 1980–1995

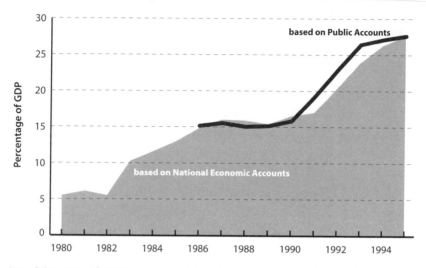

Notes: Debt series used for the provinces gives net debt, which is gross debt (total) minus financial assets. Totals include debt figures for the Canadian territories.

Sources: Gulati and Burleton, 2011; Statistics Canada, 2008, 2010e.

Figure 41: Total provincial government debt charges as a percentage of revenues, 1986/87–1995/96

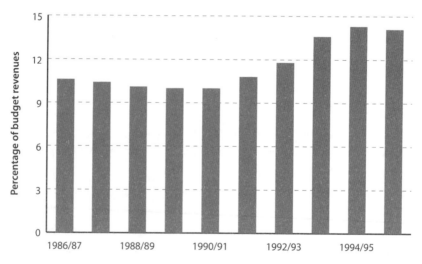

Notes: The totals include surplus and deficit figures for the Canadian territories.

Source: Canada, Department of Finance, 2010c: table 30.

Chapter 7

Understanding provincial successes of the 1990s

The 1990s were a tremendous period of reform and success in Canada. Budgets were balanced, debt was reduced, programs were reformed, taxes were lowered, and the nation's economy soared.[1] This chapter is dedicated to understanding what happened in Canada at the provincial level during this period of reform and applying those lessons to today.

Reducing spending—tackling deficits with purpose

Unlike previous periods, in the 1990s as today, there was a cascade of efforts in Canada to reduce spending in order to purposefully bring spending in line with revenues and eliminate deficits. Figure 42 illustrates the change in provincial program and total spending as a share of GDP from 1990/91 to 2006/07. Total provincial spending declined from 22.2% of GDP in 1992/93, its peak, to 18.1% of GDP in 1997/98, which represented its low point for the 1990s. It increased in 1998/99 to 18.8% of GDP, but then trended down slightly over the following decade to reach 17.9% of GDP in 2006/07. Provincial program spending, which excludes debt charges, show a similar pattern. Total provincial program spending peaked in 1992/93 at 20.0% of GDP and declined to 15.7% of GDP in 1997/98. It increased slightly over the ensuing decade to reach 16.4% of GDP by 2006/07. The key, however, as shown by both total spending and program spending in figure 42 is that spending by the provinces

---

1   For an extended discussion of this period, see Crowley, Clemens, and Veldhuis, 2010.

Figure 42: Provincial government total and program spending as a share of GDP, 1990/91–2006/07

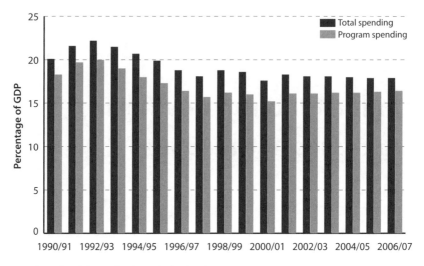

Notes: The totals include spending figures for the Canadian territories.
Source: Canada, Department of Finance, 2010c: table 31.

was reduced. To link more directly with the previous discussion, the provinces collectively reduced spending to bring their budgets into balance rather than continue to try to slow the growth in spending and while hoping that revenues would catch up.

Understanding each province's approach

There was not, however a uniform approach by the provinces and the differences among them are important to understand.[2] Table 9 summarizes the reductions in program spending enacted by the provinces during the 1990s. The figures included in the first column of data in table 9 calculate the total nominal decline in program spending from the pre-reduction peak to the post-reduction low. Also, five of the provinces implemented reductions in program spending in more than one consecutive period. The second period of decline is accounted for in the second column of data in table 9. The figures from these two columns are illustrated in figure 43.

---

2   For an overview and analysis of the spending reforms enacted in the 1990s, see Kneebone and McKenzie, 1999a, 1999b.

Table 9: Reductions in program spending, by province, 1990/91–2000/01

	Reduction in nominal program spending— first period of decline	Reduction in nominal program spending— second period of decline	Number of years of reductions in program spending, all periods	Fiscal years in which program spending declined
All Provinces	−1.3%	−2.2%	2	1993/94, 1996/97
British Columbia	−1.5%		1	1997/98
Alberta	−21.6%		3	1993/94–1995/96
Saskatchewan	−10.2%		3	1991/92–1993/94
Manitoba	−3.1%		1	1993/94
Ontario	−2.4%	−4.1%	2	1993/94, 1995/96
Quebec	−0.2%	−4.6%	3	1993/94, 1995/96–1996/97
New Brunswick	−0.9%	−3.2%	2	1993/94, 2000/01
Nova Scotia	−3.0%	−2.4%	3	1994/95–1995/96, 1997/98
Prince Edward Island	−5.0%		1	1995/96
Newfoundland & Labrador	−3.5%	−0.7%	2	1993/94, 1996/97

Sources: Canada, Department of Finance, 2010c: tables 17–26, 30; calculations by the authors.

Alberta implemented the largest reduction in program spending among the provinces. Over a three-year period from 1993/94 to 1995/96, program spending in the province was reduced by 21.6%. Saskatchewan was actually the first province to tackle its deficit through spending reductions. It implemented 10.2% reductions in program spending over a three-year period beginning in 1991/92. The remaining eight provinces all introduced reductions in program spending of less than 5.0%. Quebec (0.2%) and New Brunswick (0.9%) had the smallest reductions in program spending.

Figure 43: Reductions in program spending, by province, 1990/91–2000/01

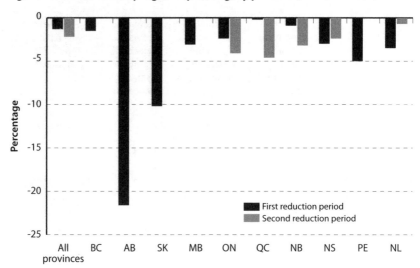

Notes: Totals include the Canadian territories. Calculations were for nominal program spending over the time period.
Source: Canada, Department of Finance, 2010c: tables 17–26, 30; calculations by the authors.

British Columbia, Manitoba, and Prince Edward Island along with Alberta and Saskatchewan were the five provinces to implement a single period of spending reductions, which spanned between one and three years. The remaining five provinces all enacted two periods of spending reductions over the course of the 1990s (table 9). For example, Quebec and New Brunswick, which had the smallest reductions in the first phase of program-spending cuts, enacted a second round of reductions in program spending of 4.6% and 3.2%, respectively.

Public sector—no sacred cows in reductions

One of the common characteristics of the spending reforms of the 1990s is that, for the most part, there were no areas of government activity that were sheltered from reform and reduction. This is best shown by the reductions in public-sector employment during this period. Many of the provincial governments that enacted reductions in public-sector employment, both directly and indirectly, maintained close ties with the labour movement in their provinces. Table 10 summarizes the decline in the number of public sector workers in each province over the 1990s. The second column shows the decline in public-sector employment during the period of reform, which is identified for each

Table 10: Reductions in provincial public-sector employment (PSE)

	1990–2000	Reductions in PSE during period of reform	Years of reductions
British Columbia	18.8%	−0.2%	1997
Alberta	−7.7%	−14.1%	1993, 1994, 1995, 1996, 1997
Saskatchewan	4.1%	−2.9%	1991, 1994, 1995, 1997
Manitoba	6.9%	−1.2%	1991, 1994, 1996
Ontario	−8.1%	−11.3%	1992, 1993, 1994, 1995, 1996, 1997, 1998, 1999
Quebec	−6.5%	−10.7%	1995, 1996, 1997, 1998, 1999, 2000
New Brunswick	−1.9%	−2.1%	1994, 1996, 1998, 2000
Nova Scotia	−6.0%	−6.2%	1994, 1995, 1996, 1997
Prince Edward Island	0.2%	−7.6%	1992, 1993, 1994, 1998
Newfoundland & Labrador	−8.9%	−8.9%	1991, 1993, 1994, 1996, 1999, 2000

Notes: Manitoba had two distinct periods of PSE reductions. The calculation in the table excludes the PSE reduction in 1991, which amounted to 1.3%. Prince Edward Island implemented a particularly deep reduction in PSE in 1998, which amounted to 8.3%. This constitutes the largest single-year reduction of any province during this decade. Public Sector Employment includes provincial and local general government, universities, hospitals and school boards. It does not include the military.
Sources: Statistics Canada, 2010f; calculations and analysis by the authors.

province in the last column. The definition of public-sector employment is a broad one that includes both provincial and local government employment as well as positions in universities, hospitals, and school boards.

Examining the entirety of the decade of reform, Newfoundland & Labrador actually implements the largest decline in the public sector (8.9%) while British Columbia experienced an 18.8% increase it is public sector employment. However, these figures simply look at the beginning of the decade compared to the end of the decade. Much more interesting and telling of the depth of reforms pursued by the provinces during this decade are the reductions that occurred during the period of reform. This more narrow measure of declines in public-sector employment indicates a period of broad austerity during which three governments enacted a reduction in their public sector in excess of 10%: Alberta (14.1%), Ontario (11.3%) and Quebec (10.7%) (table 10, figure 44). Indeed, all of the provinces except for British Columbia, Manitoba, and New Brunswick enacted fairly large decreases in their public sector employment.

Results of reform

The reductions in spending and the accordant cuts in public-sector employ-ment were not ends in themselves. Rather, they were a means by which to bring government spending in line with anticipated revenues in order to bal-ance the provinces' financial affairs purposefully and in a timely manner. The overall results were balanced or surplus budgets, declining debt, and decreas-ing interest costs.

Figure 45 illustrates the aggregate provincial surpluses and deficits from 1990/91 to 2007/08. As shown, the provinces move to an aggregate surplus position by the end of the decade, which largely lasted until the reces-sion of 2007/08. Figure 46 illustrates the individual provincial fiscal balances for 2007/08, just prior to the recession. Every province except Prince Edward Island had a surplus or a balanced budget in 2007/08.

The annual surpluses combined with a strengthening economy meant that the provinces were able collectively to reduce the size of provincial debt relative to the economy. Figure 47 illustrates the value of total provincial debt relative to GDP: provincial debt declines from a high of 29.8% of GDP in 1999/2000 to 20.6% of GDP by 2007/08.

The combination of fiscal responsibility and a general environment of low interest rates meant that the provinces enjoyed lower interest costs. Recall that lower interest costs means that there are more resources available to the government for the same amount of revenues for the purposes of program spending or tax relief. Figure 48 illustrates the consolidated provincial inter-est charges as a share of provincial budget revenues. Interest charges decline from 14.2% of consolidated provincial budget revenues in 1998/99 to 8.0% of budget revenues in 2006/07.

Figure 44: Provincial reductions in public-sector employment during various periods of reform, 1991/92–2000/01

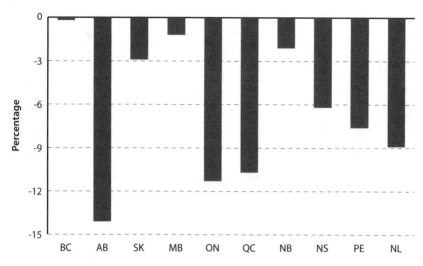

Notes: Public-sector employment includes provincial and local general government, universities, hospitals, and school boards. It does not include the military. See table 10 for details of the periods during which each province reduced public-sector employment.

Source: Statistics Canada, 2010f; calculations and analysis by the authors.

Figure 45: Total provincial government surplus or deficit as a share of GDP, 1990/91–2007/08

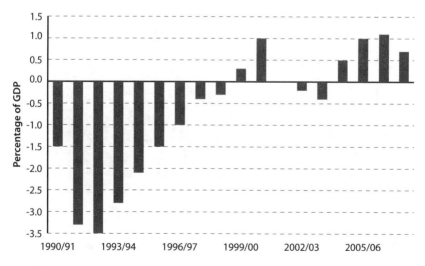

Notes: The totals include surplus and/or deficit figures for the Canadian territories.

Source: Canada, Department of Finance, 2010c: table 31.

Figure 46: Deficits and surpluses as a share of GDP, by province, 2007/08

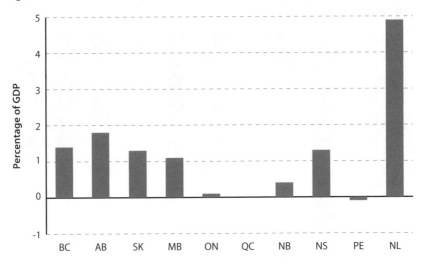

Source: Gulati and Burleton, 2011.

Figure 47: Total provincial government debt as share of GDP, 1990/91–2007/08

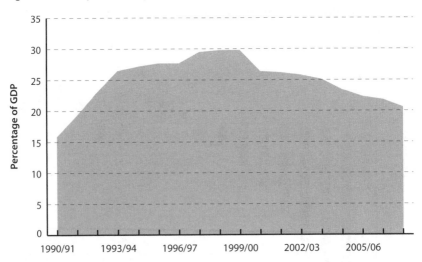

Notes: Debt series used for the provinces gives net debt, which is gross debt (total) minus financial assets. Totals include debt figures for the Canadian territories.

Sources: Gulati and Burleton, 2011.

Figure 48: Provincial government debt charges as a percentage of GDP, 1990/91–2006/07

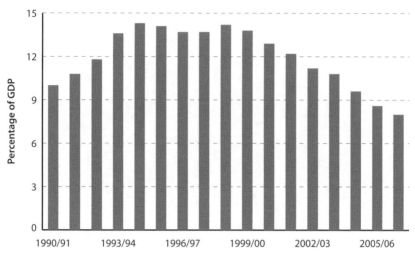

Notes: The totals include data for the Canadian territories.
Source: Canada, Department of Finance, 2010c: table 30.

Conclusion

The 1990s are an important period in Canadian political history. A number of Canadians emerged as political leaders, including Saskatchewan Premier Roy Romanow, Alberta Premier Ralph Klein, Ontario Premier Michael Harris, and other provincial leaders as well as federal leaders who changed the course of fiscal policy in Canada. These leaders rejected the failed policy of trying to slow the growth in spending and hoping that revenues would rebound sufficiently to balance their financial affairs. These leaders, which span the country geographically and politically, all implemented purposeful programs to solve their deficits. These programs varied by province but all included reducing program spending directly. In addition, all of the provinces included some cuts to the public sector as part of larger spending reduction programs. The results were stunning: provinces returned to fiscal balance and enjoyed declining debt and interest costs.

Chapter 8

Applying provincial lessons of the 1990s to today

A purposeful approach to solving a provincial deficit through spending reductions and rationalization of the public sector yields significantly better results than the approach being relied upon now by most governments, which is to slow the rate of growth in spending and wait for revenues to catch up. Provincial governments in Canada need to enact program spending reforms and reductions in order to bring their spending in line with expected revenues over the next two years, a window based on the successful experiences of Saskatchewan, Alberta, and the federal government in balancing their financial affairs in the 1990s.

British Columbia

British Columbia enjoys one of the smaller deficits (0.4% of GDP) amongst the provinces and has been on a steady track to eliminating its deficit within the next two years. The province also has one of the smaller overall debts as a share of the provincial economy but its debt has increased, in just two years, by almost 30% in nominal terms, a little over 16% as a share of the economy. As an example, taxpayer-supported debt—capital spending on hospitals, schools, and infrastructure, one of three categories of debt maintained by the province—is expected to increase by over 10% in 2011/12 alone. British Columbia should implement additional spending restraint in order to achieve a balanced budget in 2012/13, one year ahead of schedule, and ensure that capital spending returns to its historical levels, a commitment the government made in its last budget. Finally, British Columbia will have to take measured steps to ensure that its provincial debt is reduced over the next five years relative to the size of its economy.

Alberta

Alberta appears to be in one of the strongest positions amongst the provinces. After all, it is the only province without any provincial debt. While true, this masks a fairly serious financial imbalance in Alberta that must be resolved immediately. Alberta's deficit—that is spending in excess of revenues—is expected to reach $3.4 billion this year (2011/12), 1.2% of the provincial economy, and expects to remain in deficit until 2013/14. Its plan for deficit elimination, however, is highly risky. It assumes revenues will grow by over 7% while spending will be constrained to increase at 1.5%. If revenues do not grow as expected, larger deficits will persist beyond 2013/14. In addition, the marked draw-down of the province's reserve or asset accounts should be cause for great concern. Since peaking in 2009/10 at nearly $15.0 billion, the province's Sustainability Fund is expected to be no more than $5.3 billion in 2011/12, a decrease of 64.7% in two years. It is expected to decline further to $1.7 billion by 2013/14, a decrease of 88.6%. Alberta must move swiftly not only to achieve a balanced budget but also to restore the reserve accounts.

Saskatchewan

Saskatchewan is obviously in a unique and enviable position compared to the other provinces. It is the only province to have a balanced or surplus budget in 2011/12 and to expect such budgets in the future. Next to Alberta, which has no net debt, Saskatchewan has the lowest level of debt compared to the size of the province's economy: 5.7%. The challenge for Saskatchewan is two-fold. One, it needs to maintain these sound policies and not backtrack or become complacent. Two, it should forge a forward-looking set of policies to capitalize on its current financial strengths and gain real long-term advantages that foster economic prosperity. In particular, Saskatchewan needs to start thinking innovatively about how best to account for its large share of resource-related revenues. Creating an asset fund for some portion of resource revenues, particularly those from non-renewable resources would be an important first step towards creating a fiscal framework for the province that is sustainable over the long term.[1]

---

1 For an evaluation of provincial asset funds and their design, see Alberta Financial Investment and Planning Advisory Commission, 2007.

Manitoba

Manitoba is one of the middling provinces. Its current expected deficit of 0.6% of provincial GDP is one of the smaller deficits among the provinces. However, the province has only committed itself to reaching a balanced budget within three years (2014/15) and has failed to provide detailed information regarding how it plans to achieve that goal. The information that was provided indicates that the province, like too many others, will rely on strong revenue growth of 3.2% while constraining the growth in its spending to 1.8% annually. Any deviations from this plan will lead to larger immediate deficits and additional debt. The province's debt has already increased by a little over 25% in just two years to $14.8 billion, 26.2% of provincial GDP. The province would be well served by a more aggressive approach to balancing its budget and by reducing program spending this year and next.

Ontario

Ontario is still the largest provincial economy and the most populous province. However, the fiscal policies of the province are putting it in harm's way. Ontario incurred the largest deficit, both in dollar terms and as a share of the economy over the last two years and expects to record the largest deficit in 2011/12. Its current deficit of $16.3 billion or 2.6% of provincial GDP is down only slightly from last year. Ontario's deficit actually represents almost 64% of the total deficit of all the provinces in 2011/12. Perhaps more worrying is the fact that, while all the other provinces expect to reach a balanced budget either in 2013/14 or 2014/15, Ontario does not plan on reaching a balanced budget until 2017/18. And, like most other provinces, Ontario relies on revenues growing faster (4.3%) than program spending (1.4%). That means seven more years of deficits accumulating to increase the debt of the province, which is expected to reach $241.5 billion this year—or 37.8% of provincial GDP, the second highest in the country. The province's debt has increased by one quarter in just three years and its provincial debt now represents almost half of the entire stock of provincial debt in the country. The province's fiscal plan is to add significantly to that debt over the next seven years. The policy implication for Ontario is clear: a tough but realistic plan to reduce and reform spending must be implemented immediately with the specific, perhaps even sole, goal of reaching a balanced budget by 2014/15. Ontario should look not only at its own experience in the 1990s but also that of other reform-minded provinces like Saskatchewan and Alberta, as well as British Columbia in the early 2000s, to find solutions to the province's serious spending problems.

Quebec

Quebec's short-term prospects are better than Ontario's but its long-term fiscal position is the worst in the country. Quebec currently faces a deficit of nearly $3.8 billion, 1.2% of provincial GDP. It expects to balance its budget in 2013/14 but is relying on strong revenue growth (average of 4.9%) coupled with slower growth in spending (1.9%) to do so. As is the case with all the provinces relying on this passive approach, any deviation in revenues or spending will result in larger immediate deficits and greater accumulation of debt. It is this latter point that is of greatest concern. Quebec's provincial debt is already expected to reach $166.1 billion, a 10.7% increase since 2009/10. The province's debt represents over 50% of GDP, far and away the largest burden of provincial debt in the country. For instance, Quebec's provincial debt now represents 34.1% of the total stock of provincial debt while its economy only represents almost 20% of total GDP. These statistics do not include debt guarantees and similar liabilities issued by the province in mass amounts. The cost of debt, namely interest costs, are already consuming nearly 10% of revenues, which reduces the resources available for real program spending. The government of Quebec must move more swiftly to balance its budget and more importantly begin to reduce the burden of the provinces debt as a share of the provincial economy.

New Brunswick

New Brunswick's $449 million deficit, which represents 1.5% of provincial GDP, is one of the largest amongst the provinces. It does, however, represent a substantial reduction from the deficit recorded in 2009/10, which indicates the magnitude of the problem in New Brunswick. The province has committed itself to reaching a balanced budget in 2014/15 although its recent budget failed to provide any details about a plan to achieve this goal. New Brunswick's provincial debt has increased by over 20% since 2009/10 to $10.2 billion, 34.2% of GDP. While this is still manageable, the province should move more purposefully and swiftly to balance its budget and begin the process of reducing debt relative to GDP.

Nova Scotia

Nova Scotia's performance is quite mixed. It enjoyed a budget surplus in 2010/11 but slipped into a deficit in 2011/12 of roughly $390 million or about 1% of provincial GDP. Part of the explanation for the province's current deficit is the 6.8% budgeted increase in program spending for 2011/12. However, Nova Scotia is the only province to enact spending reductions (3.1%) in the next fiscal year (2012/13). Its deficit-elimination plan would yield quicker and stronger results had it avoided the large increase in program spending in 2011/12 but the province's commitment to reducing program spending and budgeting for conservative gains in revenues is a generally sound approach. The province's debt has increased only marginally since 2009/10, from $13.3 to $13.7 billion. Provincial debt, however, stands at 36.6% of provincial GDP, the third highest in the country. Interest costs now consume 10.5% of revenues in Nova Scotia, the second highest rate in the country. Nova Scotia's debt-to-GDP ratio needs to be brought down over the medium term both by controlling additions to debt and by promoting economic growth.

Prince Edward Island

Prince Edward Island, like New Brunswick, failed to provide sufficient information in its recent budget for adequate and reasonable analysis beyond the current fiscal year. The province's deficit is improving and is expected to decline to $42 million or 0.8% of provincial GDP. The commitment to achieve a balanced budget in 2014/15 is laudable but there is a lack of detail about how the province would achieve this goal and the timeline is too extended. Prince Edward Island should bring its budget into balance by 2013/14 at the latest. The province's debt has increased by almost 19% in just two years, reaching $1.9 billion in 2011/12. It is expected to reach 36% of GDP, the fourth highest rate in the country. The province needs a realistic plan to reduce its debt level relative to the size of its economy.

Newfoundland & Labrador

The province of Newfoundland & Labrador actually had a surplus last year and expects to enjoy another surplus in 2011/12. However, it expects to incur deficits of $496 million in 2012/13 (1.5% of provincial GDP) and $310 million (0.9% of provincial GDP) in 2013/14 before returning to a balanced budget in 2014/15. Provincial debt is expected to reach $8.7 billion this year, 26.7% of

GDP. While this ratio is lower than that of many provinces, it is expected to increase over the next two years as the province operates in deficit. Interest costs will consume 13.2% of revenues this year, the highest ratio of interest costs to revenues in the country. Newfoundland & Labrador should move immediately to reduce the deficits expected next year and the following by introducing spending reductions in the current year (2011/12). The 2011/12 budget indicates a reduction in program spending in 2014/15. In addition to reaching a balanced budget sooner, the province needs to make a concerted effort to reduce its stock of debt over the medium term.

Conclusion

Politicians, policy-makers, and citizens across the country need to learn the successful lessons of the 1990s and act as decisively and purposefully as those who governed in the 1990s when governments across the country of all political parties and ideologies enacted spending reductions in order to bring expenditures in line with revenues and thus achieve balanced budgets. Such actions, while difficult in the short term, lead to better results in the medium and long terms, including balanced budgets, declining debt, lower interest costs, and a more prosperous economy.

References

Alesina, Alberto, Roberto Perotti, Francesco Giavazzi, and Tryphon Kollintzas (1995). Fiscal Expansions and Fiscal Adjustment in OECD Countries. *Economic Policy* 10, 21 (October): 207–48.

Alesina, Alberto, Silvia Ardagna, Roberto Perotti, and Fabio Schiantarelli (2002). Fiscal Policy, Profits, and Investment. *American Economic Review* 92, 3: 571–89.

Barua, Bacchus, Mark Rovere, and Brett J. Skinner (2010). *Waiting Your Turn: Wait Times for Health Care in Canada: 2010 Report*. Fraser Institute. <http://www.fraserinstitute.org/uploadedFiles/fraser-ca/Content/research-news/research/publications/waiting-your-turn-2010.pdf>.

Beauchesne, Eric (1994, December 6). Reduce Debt Faster, Canada Told: Meeting Existing Target Is a Strict Minimum, OECD Warns. *Vancouver Sun*.

Boessenkool, Kenneth J. (1997). *Back to Work: Learning from the Alberta Welfare Experiment*. C.D. Howe Institute. <http://www.cdhowe.org/pdf/Kbkool.pdf>.

Canada West Foundation (1997). *Welfare Reform in Alberta: A Survey of Former Recipients*. <http://www.cwf.ca/V2/files/199713.pdf>.

Canadian Institute for Health Information (2010). *National Health Expenditure Trends, 1975–2010*. CIHI. <http://secure.cihi.ca/cihiweb/products/NHEX_Trends_Report_2010_final_ENG_web.pdf>.

Clemens, Jason, and Chris Schafer (2002). *Welfare Reform in British Columbia: A Report Card.* Fraser Institute. <http://www.fraserinstitute.org/commerce.web/product_files/WelfareReforminBC.pdf>.

Clemens, Jason, and Niels Veldhuis, eds (2007). *Beyond Equalization: Examining Fiscal Transfers in a Broader Context.* Fraser Institute

Clemens, Jason, Niels Veldhuis, and Milagros Palacios (2007). Federal Transfers and the Fiscal Balance: A Primer. *Fraser Forum* (March): 4–8. <http://www.fraserinstitute.org/uploadedFiles/fraser-ca/Content/research-news/research/articles/federal-transfers-and-the-fiscal-balance.pdf>.

Clemens, Jason, Niels Veldhuis, and Julie Kaszton (2010). *No Bang for the Taxpayer's Buck: Why California Must Reform Spending and Trim Government.* Pacific Research Institute. <http://www.pacificresearch.org/publications/no-bang-for-the-taxpayers-buck-why-california-must-reform-spending-and-trim-government>.

Crowley, Brian Lee, Jason Clemens, and Niels Veldhuis (2010). *The Canadian Century: Moving Our of America's Shadow.* Key Porter.

Elton, David (1997). *Where Are They Now? Assessing the Impact of Welfare Reform on Former Recipients, 1993–1996.* Canada West Foundation.

Emes, Joel, and Andrei Kreptul (1999). *The Adequacy of Welfare Benefits in Canada.* Fraser Institute. <http://oldfraser.lexi.net/publications/critical_issues/1999/welfare_benefits/>.

Esmail, Nadeem, and Michael Walker (2008). *How Good Is Canadian Health Care? 2008 Edition.* Fraser Institute. <http://www.fraserinstitute.org/commerce.web/product_files/HowGoodisCanadianHealthCare2008.pdf>.

Finnie, Ross, and Ian Irvine (2008). *The Welfare Enigma: Explaining the Dramatic Decline in Canadians' Use of Social Assistance, 1993–2005.* C.D. Howe Institute. <http://www.cdhowe.org/pdf/commentary_267.pdf>.

Finnie, Ross, Ian Irvine and Roger Sceviour (2005). *Social Assistance Use in Canada: National and Provincial Trends in Incidence, Entry and Exit.* Analytical Studies Research Paper no. 245 (May). Catalogue no. F0019M1E. Statistics Canada. <http://www.statcan.gc.ca/pub/11f0019m/11f0019m2005246-eng.pdf>.

Gabel, Todd, Jason Clemens, Sylvia LeRoy, and Niels Veldhuis (2003). Staying the Course on Welfare Time Limits. *Fraser Forum* (December). Fraser Institute. <http://www.fraserinstitute.org/commerce.web/product_files/FraserForum_December2003.pdf>.

Gulati, Sonya (2011a). *Give and Take to Live within Nova Scotia's Means.* TD Economics (April 5). <http://www.td.com/document/PDF/economics/budgets/td-economics-budgets-ns11.pdf>.

Gulati, Sonya (2011b). *Welcome to Life in Fiscally-Constrained New Brunswick.* TD Economics (March 22). <http://www.td.com/document/PDF/economics/budgets/td-economics-budgets-nb11.pdf>.

Gulati, Sonya, and Derek Burleton (2011). *Overview of the 2011-12 Government Budget Season: Restoring Fiscal Balance and the Plans to Get There.* Special Report (May 25). TD Economics. <http://www.td.com/document/PDF/economics/special/sg0511_budget_review.pdf>.

International Monetary Fund (2008). Fiscal Policy as a Countercyclical Tool. In *World Economic Outlook*, October 2008 (IMF): 159–96. <http://www.imf.org/external/pubs/ft/weo/2008/02/pdf/c5.pdf>.

Izumi, Lance, and Jason Clemens (2010, February 23). Learning from Canada's Schools. *Washington Times*: <http://www.washingtontimes.com/news/2010/feb/23/learning-from-canadas-schools>.

Izumi, Lance, Jason Clemens, and Lingxiao Ou (2010, July 2). What Canada Can Teach the U.S. about Education. *National Post.* Available at <http://www.pacificresearch.org/press/what-canada-can-teach-the-us-about-education>.

Karabegović, Amela, Charles Lammam, and Niels Veldhuis (2010). *Did Government Stimulus Fuel Economic Growth in Canada? An Analysis of Statistics Canada Data*. Fraser Alert. Fraser Institute. <http://www.fraserinstitute.org/research-news/display.aspx?id=15912>.

Kneebone, Ronald D., and Kenneth McKenzie (1999a). The Characteristics of Fiscal Policy in Canada. *Canadian Public Policy* 25: 483–501.

Kneebone, Ronald D., and Kenneth McKenzie (1999b). *Past (In)discretions: Federal and Provincial Fiscal Policy in Canada*. University of Toronto Centre for Public Management.

Kotlikoff, Lawrence J., and Christian Hagist (2005). *Who's Going Broke? Comparing Healthcare Costs in Ten OECD Countries*. NBER Working Paper 11833. National Bureau of Economic Research.

Kumar, Manmohan S., and Jaejoon Woo (2010). *Public Debt and Growth*. IMF Working Paper WP/10/174. International Monetary Fund. <http://www.imf.org/external/pubs/ft/wp/2010/wp10174.pdf>.

Lammam, Charles, and Niels Veldhuis (2010). Ignatieff Has It Backward on Corporate Income Taxes. *Fraser Forum* (November/December): 33–34. <http://www.fraserinstitute.org/research-news/research/display.aspx?id=16923>.

Martin, Paul (1994). *The Budget Speech*. February 22. Department of Finance Canada.

Martin, Paul (1995). *Budget Speech*. February 27. Dep't of Finance Canada.

Martin, Paul (2008) *Hell or High Water: My Life In and Out of Politics*. McClelland & Stewart.

Milke, Mark (2008). *Corporate Welfare: Now a $182 Billion Addiction. A Fiscal Update on Business Subsidies in Canada*. Fraser Alert (December). Fraser Institute. <http://www.fraserinstitute.org/research-news/display.aspx?id=12945>.

Milke, Mark (2009). *Canada's Corporate Welfare Bill: $30,252 per Family. The Justifications for Corporate Welfare Fail Again*. Frontier Centre for Public Policy. <http://www.fcpp.org/publication.php/3067>.

Murphy, Robert P., and Jason Clemens (2010). *Taxifornia: California's tax system, comparisons with other states, and the path to reform in the Golden State*. Pacific Research Institute. <http://www.pacificresearch.org/publications/taxifornia>.

Orchard, Beatrice A., and Stephen Alsford (2010). *Making Medicare: The History of Health Care in Canada, 1914–2007*. Canadian Museum of Civilization. <http://www.civilization.ca/cmc/exhibitions/hist/medicare/medic00e.shtml>.

Palacios, Milagros, and Kumi Harischandra (2008). The Impact of Taxes on Economic Behavior. In Jason Clemens (ed), *The Impact and Cost of Taxation in Canada: The Case for Flat Tax Reform* (Fraser Institute): 3–31.

Palacios, Milagros, Niels Veldhuis, and Kumi Harischandra (2008). *Canadian Government Debt 2008: A Guide to the Indebtedness of Canada and the Provinces*. Fraser Institute. <http://www.fraserinstitute.org/research-news/display.aspx?id=12881>.

Reinhart, Carmen M., and Kenneth S. Rogoff (2009). *This Time Is Different: Eight Centuries of Financial Folly*. Princeton University Press.

Richards, John (1997). *Retooling the Welfare State: What's Right, What's Wrong, What's To Be Done*. C.D. Howe Institute.

Richards, John (2000). *Now That the Coat Fits the Cloth … .* Commentary No. 143 (June). CD Howe Institute. <http://www.cdhowe.org/pdf/rich-4.pdf>.

Rovere, Mark, and Brett J. Skinner (2010). *Value for Money from Health Insurance Systems in Canada and the OECD*. Fraser Institute. <http://www.fraserinstitute.org/uploadedFiles/fraser-ca/Content/research-news/research/publications/value-for-money-health-insurance-systems.pdf>.

Roy, F. (2004). Social Assistance by Province, 1993–2003. *Canadian Economic Observer* (November): 3.1–3.7. Statistics Canada catalogue no. 11-010-XIB. <http://www.statcan.gc.ca/pub/11-010-x/11-010-x2004011-eng.pdf>.

Sabatini, E. (Rico) (1996). *Welfare—No Fair: A Critical Analysis of Ontario's Welfare System (1985–1994).* Fraser Institute.

Santayana, George (1905/1980). *Reason in Common Sense. The Life of Reason,* Vol. 1. Dover. Available at <http://www.gutenberg.org/files/15000/15000-h/vol1.html>.

Savoie, Donald J. (1999). *Governing from the Centre: The Concentration of Power in Canadian Politics.* University of Toronto Press.

Schafer, Chris, Joel Emes, and Jason Clemens (2001). *Surveying US and Canadian Welfare Reform.* Fraser Institute. <http://www.fraserinstitute.org/research-news/display.aspx?id=13457>.

Taylor, John B. (2011, January 14). Higher Investment Best Way to Reduce Unemployment, Recent Experience Shows. *Economics One: A Blog by John B. Taylor.* <http://johnbtaylorsblog.blogspot.com/2011/01/higher-investment-best-way-to-reduce.html>.

TD Economics (2009). *A Primer on Fiscal Stimulus.* <http://www.td.com/document/PDF/economics/special/td-economics-special-jm0209-stimulus.pdf>.

TD Economics (2011). *Government Budget Balances and Net Debt: As of April 11.* <http://www.td.com/economics/budgets/govt_budget_apr11.pdf>, as of April 29, 2011.

The Economist (2003, September 25). Canada's New Spirit. <http://www.economist.com>.

Veldhuis, Niels, and Jason Clemens (2003). Clarifying the Federal Government's Contribution to Health Care. *Fraser Forum* (February): 3–5. <http://www.fraserinstitute.org/research-news/research/display.aspx?id=13034>.

Veldhuis, Niels, Jason Clemens, and Milagros Palacios (2011). *Budget Blueprint: How Lessons from Canada's 1995 Budget Can Be Applied Today.* Studies in Budget and Tax Policy (February). Fraser Institute. <http://www. fraserinstitute.org/publicationdisplay.aspx?id=17269>.

Wall Street Journal (1995, January 12). Canada Bankrupt? Editorial.

Government sources

Alberta, Department of Finance and Enterprise (2011). *Budget 2011: Building a Better Alberta.* <http://budget2011.alberta.ca/>.

Alberta Financial Investment and Planning Advisory Commission (2007). *Preserving Prosperity: Challenging Alberta to Save. Report and Recommendations.* <www.finance.alberta.ca/fipac/fipac_final_report.pdf>.

British Columbia, Ministry of Finance (2011a). *Budget 2011.* <http://www. bcbudget.gov.bc.ca/2011/default.htm>.

British Columbia, Ministry of Finance (2011b). *Budget and Fiscal Plan: 2011/12 – 2013/14.* <www.bcbudget.gov.bc.ca/2011/bfp/2011_Budget_Fiscal_Plan.pdf>.

Canada, Department of Finance (1984). *The Fiscal Plan.*

Canada, Department of Finance (1985). *The Fiscal Plan.*

Canada, Department of Finance (1986). *The Fiscal Plan.*

Canada, Department of Finance (1987). *The Fiscal Plan.*

Canada, Department of Finance (1994). *Budget Plan 1994.*

Canada, Department of Finance (1995a). *Budget 1995: Facts Sheets. The Canada Social Transfer.* <http://www.fin.gc.ca/budget95/fact/FACT_10-eng.asp>.

Canada, Department of Finance (1995b). *Budget in Brief.* <http://www.fin.gc.ca/budget95/binb/brief.pdf>.

Canada, Department of Finance (1996). *Budget in Brief.* <http://www.fin.gc.ca/budget96/binb/brief.pdf>.

Canada, Department of Finance (2000). *Budget Plan 2000: Better Finances, Better Lives.* <http://www.fin.gc.ca/budget00/pdf/bpe.pdf>.

Canada, Department of Finance (2008). *Budget 2008: Responsible Leadership.* <http://www.budget.gc.ca/2008/home-accueil-eng.html>.

Canada, Department of Finance (2009). *Canada's Economic Action Plan: Budget 2009.* <http://www.budget.gc.ca/2009/pdf/budget-planbugetaire-eng.pdf>.

Canada, Department of Finance (2010a). *Budget 2010: Leading the Way on Jobs and Growth.* <http://www.budget.gc.ca/2010/pdf/budget-planbudgetaire-eng.pdf>.

Canada, Department of Finance (2010b). *Canada's Economic Action Plan: A Sixth Report to Canadians* (September). <http://www.fin.gc.ca/pub/report-rapport/2010-09-27/index-eng.asp>.

Canada, Department of Finance (2010c). *Fiscal Reference Tables.* (October) <http://www.fin.gc.ca/frt-trf/2010/frt-trf-10-eng.asp>.

Canada, Department of Finance (2010d). *Update of Economic and Fiscal Projections, October 2010.* <http://www.fin.gc.ca/ec2010/efp-pef-eng.asp>.

Canada, Department of Finance (2011). *Next Phase of Canada's Economic Action Plan—A Low-Tax Plan for Jobs and Growth* (June 6). [Update of Budget 2011, tabled March 22.] <http://www.budget.gc.ca/2011/plan/Budget2011-eng.pdf>.

Canada, Ministry of Health (2008). *Healthy Canadians: A Federal Report on Comparable Health Indicators.* Ministry of Health. <http://www.hc-sc.gc.ca/hcs-sss/alt_formats/hpb-dgps/pdf/pubs/system-regime/2008-fed-comp-indicat/index-eng.pdf>.

Canada, Ministry of Health (2009). *Canada Health Act – Annual Report 2008-09*. Ministry of Health. <http://www.hc-sc.gc.ca/hcs-sss/alt_formats/pdf/pubs/cha-ics/2209-cha-ics-ar-ra/chaar-ralcs-09-eng.pdf>.

Canada, Receiver General for Canada (2010). *Public Accounts of Canada 2010*. <http://www.tpsgc-pwgsc.gc.ca/recgen/txt/72-eng.html>.

Manitoba, Department of Finance (2011). *Budget 2011*. <http://www.gov.mb.ca/finance/budget11/index.html>.

New Brunswick, Department of Finance (2011a). *2011-2012 Budget*. <http://www.gnb.ca/0160/budget/buddoc2011/Index-e.asp>.

New Brunswick, Department of Finance (2011b). *New Brunswick Economy: 2010 in Review*. <http://www.gnb.ca/0024/index-e.asp>.

Newfoundland & Labrador, Department of Finance (2011). *Budget 2011 - Standing Strong: For Prosperity. For Our Future. For Newfoundland and Labrador*. <http://www.budget.gov.nl.ca/budget2011/default.htm>.

Nova Scotia, Department of Finance (2011). [2011-12 budget]. <http://www.gov.ns.ca/finance/en/home/budget/budgetdocuments/2011_2013.aspx>.

Ontario, Ministry of Finance (2011). *2011 Ontario Budget*. <http://www.fin.gov.on.ca/en/budget/ontariobudgets/2011/>.

Saskatchewan, Ministry of Finance (2011). *Provincial Budget 2011-12*. <http://www.finance.gov.sk.ca/budget2011-12>.

Statistics Canada (2008). *Balance Sheet of Federal, Provincial and Territorial General and Local Governments, Annual (Dollars)* [Terminated]. CANSIM table 385-0014. <http://www5.statcan.gc.ca/cansim/pick-choisir?lang=eng&searchTypeByValue=1&id=3850014>.

Statistics Canada (2010a). *Consumer Price Index (CPI), 2005 basket, annual*. CANSIM table 326-0021. <http://www.statcan.gc.ca>.

Statistics Canada (2010b). Financial market statistics (last Wednesday unless otherwise stated, monthly). <http://cansim2.statcan.gc.ca/cgi-win/cnsmcgi.exe?Lang=E&RootDir=CII/&ResultTemplate=CII/CII___&Array_Pick=1&ArrayId=1760043>.

Statistics Canada (2010c). *Estimates of population, by age and sex for July 1, Canada, provinces and territories, annual.* CANSIM table 051-0001. <http://www.statcan.gc.ca>.

Statistics Canada (2010d). *Federal, provincial and territorial general government revenue and expenditures, for fiscal year ending March 31.* CANSIM Table 385-0002. <http://www.statcan.gc.ca>.

Statistics Canada (2010e). *Provincial Economic Accounts: Data Tables.* <http://www.statcan.gc.ca/pub/13-018-x/13-018-x2010001-eng.htm>.

Statistics Canada (2010f). System of National Economic Accounts, Data Tables. <http://www.statcan.gc.ca/nea-cen/index-eng.htm>.

Prince Edward Island, Department of Finance and Municipal Affairs (2011). *2011 Provincial Budget.* <http://www.gov.pe.ca/budget/2011/index.php>.

Quebec, Department of Finance (2011). *Budget 2010-11.* <http://www.budget.finances.gouv.qc.ca/Budget/2010-2011/en/index.asp>.

United States, Congressional Budget Office [US-CBO] (2010). *Long Term Budget Outlook (June).* <http://cbo.gov/doc.cfm?index=11579>.

About the authors

Jason Clemens

Jason Clemens is the director of research at the Macdonald-Laurier Institute (MLI) and a senior fellow of the Fraser Institute. Prior to joining MLI, he was director of research at the Pacific Research Institute, a think-tank based in San Francisco. He has also held a number of positions at the Canadian-based Fraser Institute over a ten-plus year period, including the director of research quality, resident scholar in fiscal studies, and the director of strategic planning and budgeting. He has an honors B.A. in Commerce and an M.A. in Business Administration from the University of Windsor as well as a post-baccalaureate degree in Economics from Simon Fraser University.

Mr Clemens has published over 50 major studies. He has published over 250 shorter articles, which have appeared in such newspapers as the *Wall Street Journal*, *Investors Business Daily*, *National Post*, *Globe & Mail*, and all major daily papers in Canada. Mr Clemens has been a guest on numerous radio and television programs across Canada and the United States, including *ABC News*. He has appeared before committees of both the House of Commons and the Senate in Canada as an expert witness and testified before state legislatures in California. In 2006, he received the prestigious Canada's *Top 40 under 40* award presented by Caldwell Partners as well as an *Odyssey Award* from the University of Windsor.

Milagros Palacios

Milagros Palacios is a senior research economist in the Fiscal Studies Department at the Fraser Institute. She holds a B.A. in Industrial Engineering from the Pontifical Catholic University of Peru and an M.Sc. in Economics from the University of Concepción, Chile. She is co-author of *Measuring the Fiscal Performance of Canada's Premiers, Measuring Labour Markets in Canada and the United States, Fiscal Performance Index, Tax Freedom Day, Canadian Provincial Investment Climate Report, An Empirical Comparison of Labour Relations Laws in Canada and the United States, Union Disclosure in Canada and the United States, Canadian Government Debt*, and *Transparency of Labour Relations Boards in Canada and the United States*. Her recent commentaries have appeared in such newspapers as the *National Post* and *Windsor Star*. Since joining the Institute, Ms Palacios has written regularly for *Fraser Forum* on a wide range of topics, including labour regulation, fiscal issues, taxation, charitable giving, and a host of environmental issues such as air quality, Kyoto, and water transfers.

Niels Veldhuis

Niels Veldhuis is vice president of research at the Fraser Institute and one of Canada's most influential, most-read private-sector economists. As an economist, Mr Veldhuis has written five books and over 50 comprehensive studies on a wide range of economic topics including taxation, banking, productivity, investment, entrepreneurship, labour markets, and government finances. His book *The Canadian Century: Moving out of America's Shadow* is a national bestseller published by Key Porter in May 2010.

Mr Velduis is in high demand for his opinions and perspectives on major economic and social issues, appearing regularly radio and television programs across Canada and the United States. He has written over 200 articles that have appeared in over 50 newspapers including the *Globe and Mail*, *Wall Street Journal*, and *Economist*. He also writes a bi-weekly column for the *Financial Post*.

Mr Velduis is regularly asked to appear before committees of both the House of Commons and the Canadian Senate as an expert witness. He travels widely across North America, speaking to business groups, corporate gatherings, voluntary organizations and students. His speeches are humorous, educational, witty and thought-provoking.

Mr Velduis holds a Bachelor's degree in Business Administration, with joint majors in business and economics and a Master's degree in Economics from Simon Fraser University. He was recently named one of Vancouver's *Top 40 under 40* by *Business in Vancouver*.

Acknowledgments

The authors would like to thank the Fraser Institute supporters who generously provided the resources for us to undertake this study. A special thanks to Barbara and Bob Mitchell Fund and Peter Brown for their generous support of this study. In addition, we are grateful for the comments and suggestions provided by two anonymous peer reviewers.

Any errors, omissions, or mistakes remain the sole responsibility of the authors. As the authors have worked independently, the views and analysis expressed in this document remain those of the authors and do not necessarily represent the views of the supporters, trustees, or other staff at the Fraser Institute.

Publishing information

Distribution
These publications are available from <http://www.fraserinstitute.org> in Portable Document Format (PDF) and can be read with Adobe Acrobat® or Adobe Reader®, versions 7 or later. Adobe Reader® X, the most recent version, is available free of charge from Adobe Systems Inc. at <http://get.adobe.com/reader/>. Readers who have trouble viewing or printing our PDF files using applications from other manufacturers (e.g., Apple's Preview) should use Reader® or Acrobat®.

Ordering publications
For information about ordering the printed publications of the Fraser Institute, please contact the publications coordinator via:

- e-mail: sales@fraserinstitute.org
- telephone: 604.688.0221 ext. 580 or, toll free, 1.800.665.3558 ext. 580
- fax: 604.688.8539.

Media
For media enquiries, please contact our Communications Department:

- 604.714.4582
- e-mail: communications@fraserinstitute.org.
- website: http://www.fraserinstitute.org

ISBN
978-0-88975-254-2 — Printed and bound in Canada.

Date of issue
January 2012

Citation
Veldhuis, Niels, Jason Clemens, and Milagros Palacios (2012). *Learning from the Past: How Canadian Fiscal Policies of the 1990s Can Be Applied Today*. Fraser Institute.

Cover design and artwork
Bill C. Ray

Supporting the Fraser Institute

To learn how to support the Fraser Institute, please contact:

- Development Department, Fraser Institute,
  Fourth Floor, 1770 Burrard Street,
  Vancouver, British Columbia, V6J 3G7 Canada

- telephone, toll-free: 1.800.665.3558 ext. 586

- e-mail: development@fraserinstitute.org.

Lifetime patrons

For their long-standing and valuable support contributing to the success of the Fraser
Institute, the following people have been recognized and inducted as Lifetime Patrons
of the Fraser Institute.

Sonja Bata	Serge Darkazanli	Fred Mannix
Charles Barlow	John Dobson	Con Riley
Ev Berg	Raymond Heung	Catherine Windels
Art Grunder	Bill Korol	
Jim Chaplin	Bill Mackness	

Purpose, funding, and independence

The Fraser Institute provides a useful public service. We report objective information about the economic and social effects of current public policies, and we offer evidence-based research and education about policy options that can improve the quality of life.

The Institute is a non-profit organization. Our activities are funded by charitable donations, unrestricted grants, ticket sales, and sponsorships from events, the licensing of products for public distribution, and the sale of publications.

All research is subject to rigorous review by external experts, and is conducted and published separately from the Institute's Board of Trustees and its donors.

The opinions expressed by the authors are those of the individuals themselves, and do not necessarily reflect those of the Institute, its Board of Trustees, its donors and supporters, or its staff. This publication in no way implies that the Fraser Institute, its trustees, or staff are in favour of, or oppose the passage of, any bill; or that they support or oppose any particular political party or candidate.

As a healthy part of public discussion among fellow citizens who desire to improve the lives of people through better public policy, the Institute welcomes evidence-focused scrutiny of the research we publish, including verification of data sources, replication of analytical methods, and intelligent debate about the practical effects of policy recommendations.

About the Fraser Institute

Our vision is a free and prosperous world where individuals benefit from greater choice, competitive markets, and personal responsibility. Our mission is to measure, study, and communicate the impact of competitive markets and government interventions on the welfare of individuals.

Founded in 1974, we are an independent Canadian research and educational organization with locations throughout North America and international partners in over 85 countries. Our work is financed by tax-deductible contributions from thousands of individuals, organizations, and foundations. In order to protect its independence, the Institute does not accept grants from government or contracts for research.

Nous envisageons un monde libre et prospère, où chaque personne bénéficie d'un plus grand choix, de marchés concurrentiels et de responsabilités individuelles. Notre mission consiste à mesurer, à étudier et à communiquer l'effet des marchés concurrentiels et des interventions gouvernementales sur le bien-être des individus.

Peer review—validating the accuracy of our research

The Fraser Institute maintains a rigorous peer review process for its research. New research, major research projects, and substantively modified research conducted by the Fraser Institute are reviewed by a minimum of one internal expert and two external experts. Reviewers are expected to have a recognized expertise in the topic area being addressed. Whenever possible, external review is a blind process.

Commentaries and conference papers are reviewed by internal experts. Updates to previously reviewed research or new editions of previously reviewed research are not reviewed unless the update includes substantive or material changes in the methodology.

The review process is overseen by the directors of the Institute's research departments who are responsible for ensuring all research published by the Institute passes through the appropriate peer review. If a dispute about the recommendations of the reviewers should arise during the Institute's peer review process, the Institute has an Editorial Advisory Board, a panel of scholars from Canada, the United States, and Europe to whom it can turn for help in resolving the dispute.

Editorial Advisory Board

Members

Prof. Armen Alchian

Prof. Terry L. Anderson

Prof. Robert Barro

Prof. Michael Bliss

Prof. James M. Buchanan[†]

Prof. Jean-Pierre Centi

Prof. John Chant

Prof. Bev Dahlby

Prof. Erwin Diewert

Prof. Stephen Easton

Prof. J.C. Herbert Emery

Prof. Jack L. Granatstein

Prof. Herbert G. Grubel

Prof. James Gwartney

Prof. Ronald W. Jones

Dr. Jerry Jordan

Prof. Ross McKitrick

Prof. Michael Parkin

Prof. Friedrich Schneider

Prof. Lawrence B. Smith

Mr. Vito Tanzi

Past members

Prof. Friedrich A. Hayek[*†]

Prof. H.G. Johnson[*]

Prof. F.G. Pennance[*]

Prof. George Stigler[*†]

Sir Alan Walters[*]

Prof. Edwin G. West[*]

[*] deceased; [†] Nobel Laureate